Friendships That Run Deep

7 Ways to Build Lasting Relationships

Keith R. Anderson

InterVarsity Press
Downers Grove, Illinois

InterVarsity Press® is the book-publishing division of InterVarsity Christian Fellowship®, a student movement active on campus at hundreds of universities, colleges and schools of nursing in the United States of America, and a member movement of the International Fellowship of Evangelical Students. For information about local and regional activities, write Public Relations Dept., InterVarsity Christian Fellowship, 6400 Schroeder Rd., P.O. Box 7895, Madison, WI 53707-7895.

Scripture quotations, unless otherwise noted, are from the New Revised Standard Version of the Bible, copyright 1989 by the Division of Christian Education of the National Council of the Churches of Christ in the USA. Used by permission. All rights reserved.

Cover photograph: Linda Burgess

ISBN 0-8308-1966-5

Printed in the United States of America ∞

Library of Congress Cataloging-in-Publication Data

Anderson, Keith, 1949-
    Friendships that run deep: 7 ways to build lasting relationships/
Keith R. Anderson.
        p.   cm.
    Includes bibliographical references.
    ISBN 0-8308-1966-5 (alk. paper)
    1. Friendship—Religious aspects—Christianity.   I. Title.
BV4647.F7A54   1997
241'.6762—dc21   97-12918

CIP

21 20 19 18 17 16 15 14 13 12 11 10 9 8 7 6 5 4 3 2 1

15 14 13 12 11 10 09 08 07 06 05 04 03 02 01 00 99 98 97

*To my father
in his eightieth year
—a lifetime
of wisdom and integrity*

Acknowledgments

This book began as an ongoing discussion in the living room of one of life's great gifts: Jennifer Pryor. She assembled a focus group that included other creative and helpful people whom I am pleased to call my friends: Chris Petersen, Laura Slaikeu, Kip Johannsen, Julie Rittgers, Andi Anderson and Scott Pearcy. My thanks to Anne Johanssen, whose careful reading caught many errors.

I am especially grateful to my editor, Cindy Bunch-Hotaling, whose wise guidance has led me through three books and who, through this process, has become a good friend.

A book on friendship is a risky project to bring to publication because it cannot honor all of the people I have been privileged to know as friends or to recount all the ways my friends have taught me what I write in this book. To all my friends I can only say: You have taught me much through your patience, challenge and love; thank you.

With some of you I have had especially provocative conversations about friendship in many settings: Kirby Wilcoxson, Randy Reese, Ron Hagele, Steve Young, Jim Koch and Dave Brandt. I will always cherish our rich conversations.

One

The Hospitality of Friendship

There is no possession more valuable than that of a
good and faithful friend.
S O C R A T E S

*T*HE CLOUDS OVERHEAD SWIRLED ANGRILY IN THE CHURN-
ing gray sky. Indifferent to the insult, large drops of rain slapped
the cars below as they wound through the roads in silent single
file and stopped in order at the edge of the cemetery. I watched,
intensely interested in the faces of people. Silent of voice and grim
of spirit they were; I lifted my collar to repel the assault of the
bitter wind and felt the iciness of cold wet feet. Sadness and anger,
the twin voices of human grief, were present at the graveside. The
crowd swelled in numbers, people drawing ever closer, needing
something that had to be shared in that moment and at that place.

Six men stood most erect and steeled their faces against their
own hearts, certainly against the tears that clamored for release.
I was their pastor but they were his closest friends. His death
struck them with the pain of irreversible reality: he was gone. I
read my words, but only these men could unveil the feelings from
deep within hearts anguished by his death.

As I watched them leave the cemetery, a voice within wondered, *What is this power, this force, this sacred love which draws people together with such profound and wonderful depth that, even in the moment of death's agonizing pain, people stand together in bitterly cold rain to say goodby . . . to their friend?* My hands clutched the coffee cup, more for its warmth than its refreshment, and I let my mind wander to a mental scrapbook of faces and names, people I have known, friends I have had and lost. At the funeral earlier in the day, an old man whom I did not know walked past the open casket and leaned forward, hot tears burning his face as he kissed the hand of one he had known for decades. Later, he stammered out these poignant words: "He was my friend."

On that day I started a quest to understand the human love we call friendship. I don't know if I can write about it, but I can recognize it when I see it. I don't know if this attempt to describe and explain what I have learned will articulate it, but I know it when it stands before me in the form of human eyes and heart and life. Although it is impossible to "capture," perhaps it is possible to slow down the motion of friendship enough to see it more clearly.

The Quest to Understand Friendship

Friendship is something we have all had but will never exhaust, something we don't need in order to live and breathe but something we cannot live without. We both give it away and receive it. It can both heal and hurt. It is not dependent on age, gender, race, religion, geography or creed.

In a biological sense we don't need friendship in order to survive, but we know that we cannot live fruitfully without it. It is a force that is present in every part of the world, a power that has emerged in every generation, culture and place, a dynamic that has animated people in all ages of human history. Eavesdrop on conversations at coffee shops, restaurants, kitchen tables, dormitories, offices, factories or in cars, airplanes and buses and sooner or later the word will find its way into the conversation. "I have a friend who..." "My friend and I..." "I don't understand my friend; she . . ." "I am angry at my friend because he . . ." Friendship is a *fact* of life, and it is a *puzzle* in life.

Some attempt to define friendship functionally and propose that friendships are built on the basis of three "rewards." In this understanding, friendship is something we "do" or "have" in order to achieve a personal reward:

1. instrumental rewards such as advice, money or shared work

2. emotional rewards such as support and encouragement

3. shared interest rewards such as companionship or common values

Christians understand that friendship is a reflection of the image of God we carry within ourselves. To be created in the image of God means that we are created for love and relationship, in other words, for friendship. As the divinity of God is alive in the community of the Trinity, so we are created for relationships with one another. It is the great spiritual mystery of our humanness. We cannot be fully human apart from one another. We were *created* for relationship. It is not merely an instinct or an animal drive within; we are stamped with the character of God by our creation in a way that compels us to seek relationships for our souls just as we seek oxygen for our lungs. Without friendship, we are less than fully human, so we seek relationships with others to fill that inner longing for completion, companionship and wholeness. We may not be able to articulate what drives us but we "know" it intuitively.

Some point out that friendship is the ancient drive to love and be loved—what early generations called "eros." Alan Jones explains, "*Eros* is not simply the drive towards sexual fulfillment; it is the impulse towards any satisfaction and completion. . . . Love in this sense is much more than a romantic urge. It is the desire of every creature to find its proper place, to find its true home."[1]

Sooner or later we recognize that we are human in relationship to one another; we are drawn toward one another by an innate need as powerful as the sexual drive of a man for a woman or a woman for a man. We cannot be fully alive, fully human persons apart from others. We need others to help us fully live "at home" in the universe and in our smaller, more personal worlds. We crave relationships because they reflect an essential part of our makeup as human persons. We are relational people who are fulfilled in life, in large measure, based on the quality of our relationships, especially friendships.

Frederick Buechner's insight comes close to what I feel when I try to describe friendship.

Friends are people you make part of your life just because you feel like it. There are lots of other ways people get to be part of each other's lives like being related to each other, living near each other, sharing special passion with each other like P.G. Wodehouse or jogging or lepidopterology, and so on, but though all of those may be involved in a friendship they are secondary to it.

Basically your friends are not your friends for any particular reason. They are your friends for no particular reason.[2]

The Confusion About Friendship

Feeling something between anger and simmering frustration, he sat across from me and said, "Let's get real—friendship is not easy. It is not neat and tidy. I've had good friends and I've had bad friends. I've known friends who would give me the shirt off their backs and others who would just as soon stab me in the back. Friendship is confusing. Being a friend is difficult. Having and keeping friends is complicated."

I couldn't agree with him more, which is why I have written this book. I have not had great success in all my friendships. Some

have been marked by a disappointing no and some by an inde-
scribable yes. I have tasted the rich joy of good friendship enough
to keep me coming back to the table for more. We have all failed
in friendships before. They are too human, too real, too clumsy,
too unwieldy to fit into easy descriptions, formulas or lists of rules.

For two years in junior high school I tagged around after Mike,
trying desperately to make him accept me as a friend. He tolerated
me, nothing more. Before that I stood in the sixth-grade shadow
of Randy, hoping he would notice my loyalty and invite me into
the inner circle as one of "the guys." When he became captain of
the patrol boys, I saw my chance and asked him to make me his
lieutenant. He laughed; I didn't.

Like all of us, I know the pain of friendships that never got
started or that soured in the passing of time. I know the stabbing
pain of rejection and the hollow sadness of indifference.

In my more than twenty years of working with people in many
different settings, I have watched them struggle with friendship.
Here's what some of them have said.

☐ I'm pretty good at meeting new people and getting conversations going, but I don't seem able to move past the superficial to
the deep.

☐ I don't have people I consider truly close friends like I did when
I was in college. After graduation most of my friendships changed
and we drifted apart. Now I wonder: will I ever again know the
rich feel of truly close friends?

☐ My friendships are good for a while, and then it seems something happens to disrupt them or to make them go bad. I feel like
there is something missing in my approach to friends that hinders
me from keeping friendships going. What am I missing?

☐ I live most of my life in a world full of strangers. I know people
where I work and where I worship, but I can't honestly say I ever
feel that I am known by anyone else.

☐ My friends have all gotten married, and I feel left behind in the dust as they race off into their busy and happy futures. When we get together I am the fifth wheel on the car and feel patronized by people who used to be my best friends.

☐ Friendships, for me, are like the holidays. After all the noise and excitement, all you have left is empty wrapping paper.

☐ There has been nothing singularly more damaging in my life than my friendships. Friendship has significant power to hurt. I am tired of the trivialization of friendship that I see on TV and in magazines, bored with the sentimentalization of friendship I see in movies and novels. Where are the people who will tell the truth about friendship? It can hurt, deeply.

Curiosity About Friendship

What is this thing that can hurt so deeply and yet elate so joyously? To be honest, my scrapbook of friends isn't filled with exclusively happy *or* sad photos, but memories of both. I might show you my scars from the wounds inflicted by hurtful friends over the years, but I might also want to open the scrapbook of memories and tell you stories of a few others whose friendship can never be adequately described or extolled. For starters, let me tell you about my friend Kirby.

He's a Hoosier; I'm an Illini. I grew up believing that the corn grew taller, the women more beautiful, the men more handsome and life more sophisticated on the west side of that border. He had the presence of mind to speak kind and affirming words after a chapel message, and I knew I could forgive him for being born on the wrong side of that state line. Thirteen years later he knows me and I him. When we meet several times each year, we talk; we speak our hearts and minds to one another. We trust. We confront. We go deep. We love. I don't know anyone who has frustrated me more than him. I don't know anyone more opposite from me than him. And I don't know anyone I trust with my soul more than him.

Dramatic, dangerous, battlefield situations? Is that what bound us together as friends? Did he save my family from a burning building, or did I rescue his dog from a runaway car? Did friendship grow through earth-shattering, life-transforming, sensational and spectacular events in life? No. It came through working together, competing together, eating together, praying together, worshiping together, laughing together, crying together, doubting together, believing together, failing together, winning together, growing together.

As I researched and prepared to write this book, I became particularly interested in *how we think* about friendship and how our thinking affects the way we act in those relationships. While many books discuss the *skills* of friendship, few seem focused on understanding what this thing is that weaves its way through every era and facet of our lives. I have learned the importance of looking at the lens we use for viewing friendship because it will tint the way we see what friendship is and how it works in our lives. Our perspectives on friendship shape our expectations, which in turn determine to a large extent the success or failure of our relationships.

As children we are unfocused and indiscriminate in our thinking: if you will like me, you can be my friend; if you will play with me, I will be yours. A friend is someone who is here now and willing to play life's games with me. The time comes, however, when a gray cloud covers the sky and a painful reality descends on our naiveté and innocence. We need more than indiscriminate playmates, more than temporary diversions; we need someone whose love will reflect a bright and warm light to us in the cloudiness of life. A friend is someone who comes alongside, stands alongside, stays alongside. There is a clumsy clamoring for synonyms for friendship. "He's like a brother to me." "We are closer than sisters." "They are inseparable."

Friends are people we have just met, and they are people we

have loved all of our lives. As a word standing on its own, *friendship* can mean little or much, but when the tender bruise of loneliness throbs, we know what friendship is, whether the words suffice or not.

The Hospitality of Friendship

I sat across from a friend at lunch, letting the conversation follow its own lively and natural will. There were moments of honesty and self-disclosure between us, and then he mused, "Do you know what I need from my friends? When my life gets blurred by 'too much' and 'too many,' I just need someone to reflect God's light back to me and turn God's mirror back on me so I can remember I am valued."

So I am convinced it is inadequate to merely provide lists of friendship skills, qualities of good friends or descriptions of successful friendships without trying at least to draw a sketch of the essential nature of friendship.

What is friendship? In this book I will suggest a provocative metaphor that will help us understand the essential nature of friendship as well as provide practical steps for working with friendship. It is the metaphor of hospitality.

In his book *Reaching Out,* Henri Nouwen talks about the rich concept of hospitality as *the process of creating a free and open space in which people can meet without fear or hostility.* He reminds us that hospitality is one of the fundamental biblical practices expected of those who take biblical teachings seriously.

Although many, we might even say most, strangers in this world become easily the victim of a fearful hostility, it is possible for men and women and obligatory for Christians to offer an open and hospitable space where strangers can cast off their strangeness and become our fellow human beings. . . . That is our vocation: to convert the *hostis* into a *hospes,* the enemy into a guest and to create the free and fearless space where brotherhood and sisterhood can be formed and fully experienced.[3]

As we begin this conversation, I offer Nouwen's image of hospitality as a practical working definition of friendship that is textured enough to be worth our time and energy. *Friendship is creating hospitality; it is creating a free and open space where we can receive each other as a gift for our lives.*

I invite you to think about your current relationships and see if you agree: are you able to see your friendships as opportunities for giving and receiving the welcome grace of another's hospitality? *Friendship is creating hospitality; it is creating a free and open space where I can receive another as a gift for my life.*

Hospitality can help us understand the practical workings of friendship more readily. Some people are not good hosts. Some are too busy to be thoughtful hosts. Some are so preoccupied with their own lives that they are distracted as hosts. And some are just too wrapped up selfishly in their own agendas to be helpful hosts. Hospitality is both as uniquely personal as the individual and also broadly universal, which means it can be learned by anyone but is an art more naturally and skillfully practiced by some.

Sometimes friendship crosses lines of age. One of the earliest memories I have of friendship involves an elderly man in my church, Mr. Wittoff. I was only about four or five but found clever and sometimes devious ways to get away from my parents and slip into the seat next to "my friend." I have no idea how the ritual started, but I have clear and very warm memories of climbing into the welcoming arms of Mr. Wittoff. Occasionally I even got to sit with him for the entire church service.

What did he do? He was decades older than me. We had very little in common. He didn't like to play the games that I did, and I'm certain I couldn't understand his adult conversations, but he offered me what I needed most then: a welcoming and gracious invitation to sit with him. He literally created a free and open space for me to be. I loved Mr. Wittoff and felt genuine sadness when we moved away from that church. He offered me hospitality in a way a preschool child could understand.

Sometimes friendship crosses lines of culture and background. Wendy and Lachschmi worked together in a large insurance company office. Wendy is a middle-class woman from "middle America," daughter of a managerial-level father who worked for a major U.S. manufacturing company and a homemaker mother. She grew up as a Baptist. Lachschmi grew up in India, daughter of parents of the Hindu religion. Each day she appeared at the office dressed in a sari, an obvious sign of her culture. In distinct ways her Hindu faith was evident as well.

A warm friendship developed that crossed lines of geography, religion, economics, background and culture. Each created hospitality and offered a free and friendly space for the other, a welcoming place of communication, mutual respect, affection, trust and certainly curiosity about cultural differences.

I think Jesus would appreciate the image of friendship as hospitality because he valued relationships so highly. His earthly ministry began with friendship. He gathered a small community of people around him to learn from him, to share with him, to enjoy life together with him and to begin the work of building a new world. In John 13:34-35 we read his words: "I give you a new commandment, that you love one another. Just as I have loved you, you also should love one another. By this everyone will know that you are my disciples, if you have love for one another."

I sat back one day and pondered the meaning of those words. In effect Jesus said, "I *command* you to have relationships in which you act for the well-being of others. People will know that you are my students if you have relationships with others." I then thought about those words in terms of friendship. Think how those verses sound if for the words of love we substitute the words of friendship: "I give you a new commandment, that you become friends with one another. Just as I have been your friend, you also should be friends with one another. By this everyone will know that you are my disciples, if you have good friendships with one another."

Near the end of his ministry, Jesus said something like that when he talked of his disciples and declared them his friends in a statement unparalleled by a first-century rabbi. His students were revisioned—no longer as servant-learners but strikingly transformed as friends: "I do not call you servants any longer, because the servant does not know what the master is doing; but I have called you friends, because I have made known to you everything that I heard from my Father. You did not choose me but I chose you" (Jn 15:15-16).

Jesus carefully selected the metaphor of friendship after he had taught them as mentor and rabbi. No longer were his followers to be seen in a narrowly defined role; now Jesus invites them to move with him into the broad uncharted territory of friendship. Just as he dramatically offered a new metaphor for God—*abba* or "dear Father," a term of intimate affection—he recast his metaphor for his learners as *friends*. Both are terms of relationship, of affection, of familiarity, of intimacy.

Isn't that what we all long for and desire, to find friends who will reflect Jesus' own high value of friendship to us? Friendship is one way we give and receive love. It is a vehicle through which love is channeled, a vehicle that can get blocked or flow freely. It is a container of grace and a pathway for that grace to be expressed.

I write from a deep and certain conviction: God has given friendship to the human family as a means of grace. Friendship is sacramental in the sense that God cares about friendship, honors it and shows us love through numerous human relationships.

In this book we will share a conversation about the confusing, complicated, sometimes difficult phenomenon of friendship. I am convinced the conversation can help us all deepen, enrich and develop our friendships.

As I started to write this book I took a tour through Scripture to see if, where and how friendship was present in it. You may be as surprised as I was to find a continual theme of friendship. Although there are many biblical friendships, I have become convinced that several of them invite us to experience best the teaching of God's Word about our subject. I have identified biblical stories and poems in the Old and New Testaments that show us seven important perspectives on friendship.

This book doesn't offer formulas or easy answers to complex matters of friendship but is written in the belief that the search for understanding is worth the struggle. Any book or article that offers you five easy steps to the perfect relationship is not worthy of your time. Friendship is as unique and original as you are. Friendships come in all sizes, shapes, languages, cultures and styles. What works in one relationship may not work in another. What is meaningful in your friendships may not have the same value for another. Yet all of us seem to share a natural curiosity about friendship and a hunger for a relationship with at least one other human being who will walk with us on the journey. I will not insult you by suggesting that I have "answers" for your questions or solutions to all of your problems. I don't, but I believe there is value in a shared conversation, which is the way I have written this book. Welcome.

Study Questions

1. Who was your best friend when you were eleven? What made that friendship so important to you?

2. Who is your "best" friend today? What makes that person important to you?

3. What are three reasons you seek out others as friends? What are you looking for in a good friend?

4. What prompted you to read this book? Why now?

5. Take an inventory of your current friendships. Are they healthy and strong? What areas can you identify that need growth?

Two

If You Really Knew Me

A friend is a person with whom I may be sincere.
Before him, I may think aloud.
EMERSON

Friendship requires the choice of unmasking.

SHE SAT IN THE CIRCLE WITH SIX OTHERS IN THE CLASS. I asked what I thought was a harmless question, an ice-breaker, a discussion starter: "Finish this sentence any way you wish: 'If you really knew me . . .' "

Pete started. "If you really knew me, you'd want to talk to me about cars. I love cars, especially racing." Dana was next. "If you really knew me, you'd know that I grew up in the mountains and love to hike every chance I get."

It was going well. We were learning some things that would help the group bond and would help us move ahead into the deeper levels of conversation in the course.

Sarah was the last to speak. She looked down and fumbled with her watch, twisting it around her wrist in a methodical motion, pausing a long time between words. She sighed deeply, frequently and slowly before she spoke. Her words came out in the hollow tone of one whose pain was deep and detached. "If you really knew me," she said. "If you really knew me . . . If you really knew me you wouldn't like me."

The harmless ice-breaker had unearthed an iceberg of emotion and pain. Six people spoke of safe and superficial things; one bared her pain. Six people played the game of relationships, while one anguished over an essential human fear: If you really knew me, you wouldn't like me, let alone accept me or treasure me.

Paul Tournier has a valuable way of speaking about the first of our seven biblical teachings on friendship. He distinguishes between the *person* and the *personage*. The *person* is one's truest self, the inner me, the unvarnished and unadulterated self. It is that internal sense of self that is most personal, private and protected. The *personage*, on the other hand, is the persona; it is the public self, the "me" that others see, the "me" that I believe myself to be, the image of myself that I present to you, the face that I show you in public, official or projected ways. It is the mask that I wear in safety.

Tournier says the personage operates much like a city or country that is presented for public show at times of pageantry or display. As I write this chapter, Atlanta is hosting the Summer Olympic Games. City officials have put the best face on the city and are presenting it as a cultured, civilized, organized and controlled metropolis. Just a few months ago, however, the "shadow self" of Atlanta was seen in acts of violence, racism and ugliness. Indeed, the violence of bombing marred the festive spirit of the games themselves. That, Tournier would say, is part of the true self. The personage is the mask we wear to protect the safety of the person within. But the first biblical perspective teaches us that *friendship requires the choice of unmasking.*

In the early stages of a developing friendship we decide what to do with the masks we wear. Will we reveal our truest self to another? Will we open our deepest feelings to another or protect ourselves with caution and safety? Will we wear our masks or take the risk of unmasking with another human being? Jerry and Mary White identify three levels of friendships with people.

Level One: Casual friends are acquaintances, people we see regularly in casual social contacts. We may know these people for a short time or a lifetime, but we seldom go deep with them.

Level Two: Close friends are people with whom we share an important activity, project or function such as organizations, churches, study or service organizations. We develop a consistent relationship with these people.

Level Three: Intimate friends are the small inner circle of people "to whom we pour out our souls, sharing our deepest feelings and hopes. They meet us at our point of deepest need, and we enjoy and look forward to being with them above all others."[1]

The Whites' description shows us that not all friendships are the same, for intimacy and commitment vary. Not all friendships will run deep, become vulnerable and nurture our souls. This is an important truth: there are levels to friendship. The level to which we go depends in large measure on the act or acts of unmasking.

Friendship requires the choice of unmasking. It is learning to be vulnerable or what has been called "the art of self-disclosure." The word *vulnerable* means "unprotected, subject to attack, defenseless, open to danger." It is what happens when I take off the mask of my *personage* in order to reveal and share the *person* within; I become vulnerable to the danger of another person. This is not a risk to be taken lightly, as our own experiences have taught us: vulnerability can cause pain.

David and Jonathan

The story of David and Jonathan covers dozens of verses and many pages in the Bible. It is a wonderful picture of two men who grow through many progressive stages of friendship, but the beginning of their friendship offers a particularly striking picture of vulnerability and of a conscious decision to unmask.

Jonathan was the son of the powerful first king of Israel, Saul; he was the prince of the royal first family of the nation. By contrast, David was the son of a shepherd, a farmer named Jesse, the youngest son at that, least in the lineage of his family tree. The social distinction was marked—the royalty of one stands in direct contrast to the commonness of the other. David had just finished his famous battle with the Philistine giant, Goliath, and was brought into the audience of the king to report on his victory. As he answered Saul's questions, he described his humble background as a shepherd in Bethlehem.

The young prince, Jonathan, watched David tell his story to the king. First Samuel 18:1 says, "When David had finished speaking to Saul, the soul of Jonathan was bound to the soul of David, and Jonathan loved him as his own soul." It began as many friendships do—with an unscheduled, chance encounter that creates a curiosity or an interest in the other. There was "chemistry," a natural interest in or attraction to the other that led to friendship. It is probably not possible to explain why we like every individual to whom we are attracted or in whom we are interested. It just happens.

Jonathan, however, took it further in a step of vulnerability toward his social "inferior," thus illustrating the principle of unmasking: "Then Jonathan made a covenant with David, because he loved him as his own soul. Jonathan stripped himself of the robe that he was wearing, and gave it to David, and his armor, and even his sword and his bow and his belt" (1 Sam 18:3-4).

A covenant is an agreement between two parties, which was commonly used in the ancient world for political, legal and military purposes. It was an attempt to define and describe the relationship between two parties. Sometimes it was used in a more personal setting to interpret and make agreements between two individuals such as Jonathan the prince and David the shepherd. Jonathan made the first move to set aside any worries that David might have about a social gap between them. After all, Jonathan was the son of the king and David was merely the servant of the king. Jonathan took the step of vulnerability toward David and showed his friendship in a tangible and practical covenant of friendship. Later covenants between these two men would establish protection for Jonathan's children, but this agreement seems to be a covenant of friendship.

An exchange of weapons like this was an ancient way of sealing a friendship. When he gave David his *robe* he offered him a relationship of equals—he took off the mask of royal power and authority, placing himself on a level plane with David. When he took off his *armor* he removed the mask of defense, placing himself on an unprotected level with David—he became truly vulnerable. When he handed over his *sword and bow*, he removed the mask of weapons and literally disarmed himself, placing himself in a posture of nondefensiveness. When he offered David his *belt* he apparently gave David access to some of Jonathan's authority to the throne.

The symbolism is stunning: no obvious signs of superiority, no defensiveness, no ability for attack, and access to the same authority and power. The cultural and historical differences between the ancient world and ours are many. I'm not suggesting that we simply ignore them, but we should look at Jonathan's initiative as a wonderful metaphor for the step all friends must take at one time or another, that of unmasking. Jonathan set aside his power and status to invite David into his world through a vulnerable act of unparalleled hospitality. The writers of the text seem insistent that we see it clearly: Jonathan intentionally unmasked himself because of his desire for friendship with David. Friendship begins with the step of unmasking, of disarming, of offering oneself in vulnerability to another. Jonathan's symbolic gifts can be understood as tangible expressions of inner feelings of openness. Despite his status and place as the prince, son of a powerful monarch, Jonathan readily set aside all of that in order to gain the friendship of David.

Friendships start most often when someone "makes the first move" of vulnerability toward another. It becomes a guessing game unless the other responds in kind with a reciprocal move of interest, but someone has to take that first step through the risk of unmasking. I believe that unmasking is contagious; there is no substitute for straightforward candor in the early days of a relationship. Nothing will move the relationship forward as quickly as such transparency.

Will You Be My friend?

As young children we often start the friendship cycle indirectly, shyly or coyly. "Do you want to play catch with me?" "I have two shovels; do you want to dig in the sand with me?" "Let's go ride bikes together." Or, "Do you want to come to my house and play?" As we mature we find more sophisticated ways to share our toys, shovels and time, but the risk of unmasking is only increased.

Think back to an early childhood friendship. How did it get started? Who made the first move? What happened next? Now think about a more recent adult friendship. How did it get started? Who made the first move? In what sense did it involve the art of unmasking?

They sat across from one another in a restaurant, a very public place filled with noise and traffic. People were coming and going, and the din of clattering plates was erratic and distracting. "How are you?" she asked, intending only a superficial and casual meaning.

"I am fine," came the response, though her table partner felt uneasy and scared. "I'm not very good at this," she continued, looking down at her fingernails and then glancing around the room to see how long she had before the waitress returned. "In fact, I'm not very good at this at all. Friendships are hard for me, but I feel like we have a lot in common and it seems like this could grow into something significant."

The awkwardness didn't pass, but there was something more relaxed about the moment. The risk had been taken!

Unmasking can be as emotion-charged as that or as simple as "Hey, let's go get a cup of coffee," but it starts with the initiative of unmasking. Unless we learn the art of unmasking, potential friends will remain acquaintances and nothing more. Acquaintances are people whom we know from a distance, sharing little of ourselves. Friendships that run deep require honesty with others and learning to set aside the pretensions that we often use to protect ourselves. Dare to open up! It's not a formula for friendship, but it is a necessary step.

In Genesis 2:25 we see another description of this principle of vulnerability: "And the man and his wife were both naked, and were not ashamed." They stood before each other with nothing between them, and they felt no shame. Their nakedness was not physical only; it is a metaphor that speaks of openness, honesty and integrity. In God's original design there was no need for fig leaves; in fact, in God's original design there was no need for cover-ups of any kind. Two people stood before each other and could relate in the freedom of honesty, without shame. There was no need for the suspicious and calculating manipulation we think of as normal. One person could relate to another person in innocent vulnerability—nothing to hide, nothing to protect.

One commentator has said, "Once people could stand unembarrassed before the gaze of God." Is that merely a faint memory, told only in stories of a past now impossible to recover? I have become convinced that friendship offers a doorway into the realm of deeply trustful honesty.

Relationships cannot move beyond basic acquaintance without at least some baby steps of transparency. Relationships wither and die when openness goes out of them or when double-talk becomes the normal mode of communication—when all of our words become couched in double meanings and we have to think carefully to protect our secrets. How does that happen to us? How do we move from this free and open honesty to a point where we continually need to hide behind the fig leaves of fear, dishonesty and shame?

Hide and Seek

Can you remember, as a child, playing the game of hide-and-seek, that delightful pastime of running, hiding and then waiting to be discovered? You stood or crouched in some corner, almost panicked that you'd be discovered and still almost more afraid that you might not.

And can you remember that time as a child when you were honest and open with someone and they used your secrets to hurt you? And the promise that you made with yourself to be more careful with your feelings next time—to play hide-and-seek with those feelings, to protect yourself against being hurt? Soon we live in two worlds—one is the world that people see and hear, the other is where our true feelings are hidden away in a safe vault, protected against unkind or hurtful words and actions from so-called friends.

By the time we arrive at adulthood our growth is stunted or we have lost the ability to be open with another. We have learned to be cautious and protective of our vulnerable inner person because of damage, real or perceived, from ungracious hospitality in our lives.

There appears to be a pertinent gender difference worth noting at this point, at least in Western cultures. Men seem less capable of comfortably practicing this art of unmasking, while women seem more readily able to unmask with several friends at the same time. Add to this another serious factor heavily supported by recent research: men tend to have more superficial relationships than women and find honest, open communication to be difficult.

Letty Cottin Pogrebin observes, "Time and again, researchers have come up with the same results: Men have *more* friends than women but women's friendships are richer, deeper, and more meaningful. Let's put it this way: If friendship were a course of study, men would get 'incomplete' in four significant subjects."[2] She goes on to identify those four areas of "incomplete" in men's relationships with men:

☐ Men do not give each other affection

☐ Men do not talk to other men about intimate things

☐ Men do not nurture each other

☐ Men do not have holistic friendships. They tend to see each other as persons filling particular roles.[3]

What all this suggests is that men struggle with the spiritual battle of pride. Men are afraid to not be in control, so they act as if their world is okay even if it is falling apart. To show emotion openly to others is to show weakness, and in Western cultures weakness is not considered a positive trait for men. The result is a superficial level of communication and an unwillingness to confess or forgive.

I was fascinated by this interpretation from Pogrebin: "Women talk about themselves, their feelings, doubts, fears, love relationships, families, homes, and problems; men talk about competition and aggression, and things they have seen or heard. They discuss work, sports, politics, social issues, money, business, cars, weather, and traffic. . . . Whatever the ostensible subject of men's talk—sex, sports, politics—it is really about proving one's manhood and ending up on top."[4]

"Ending up on top" is a formula for spiritual pride; it will keep you from that which you need the most—confession and forgiveness through mutual friendship. It leads to the strategy of denial, avoidance and dishonesty; it is a strategy that may lead to bitterness or the loss of the friendship. The better strategy is to learn to unmask, to practice it and to learn it on the way, by taking the risks as so many are willing to do in competitive sports, business and other enterprises.

There is no way to develop deep friendships without cultivating the art of unmasking.

Boundaries and Discernment

"Isn't that kind of friendship risky and dangerous? Should I just open up to everyone and anyone?" The person's questions were honest and apparently rooted in a history of rejection.

"Discernment is the opposite of foolhardy recklessness," I said. "Be careful and selective with your risk taking."

The book of Proverbs says, "Some friends play at friendship but a true friend sticks closer than one's nearest kin" (18:24). The principle of unmasking has to do with *choice*. There are some friends who bring you to ruin and others who bring to you the richness and prosperity of love. Wise discernment is needed but can be learned only through practice.

It is good to speak honestly of the risks of friendship. There are what Nouwen called "small rejections of everyday" that can cause us pain. Especially prevalent today is the unintended hurt from sarcastic humor or the sudden paper cut of a hurtful flippant remark. There can be the brisk denial or bitter silence from someone whose intentions were purely innocent but whose words brought us pain. In a world where words are trivialized by their abundance and the sarcasm of comedic language, we are prone to misuse words in ways that will hurt.

Boundaries are therefore necessary for our mental and personal health. People who are open to everyone about the most personal and intimate details of life are not psychologically healthy. Their socialization has been inadequate or failed; they do not have a clear sense of their own identity and thus share freely with everyone. A healthy person has a healthy sense of psychological and personal boundaries and an ability to say, "No, this part of me is private, to be shared only with a trusted friend." Boundary making is an essential part of unmasking.

I watched Shannon stumble her way through her first three painful years of college. If anyone looked her way or smiled as she passed, she took it as a sign of friendship. There was a desperation, an urgency in her need for people to like her, and she made indiscriminate choices. Anyone who showed interest in her could talk her into almost anything.

I found her one winter's day under a stairwell in a remote part of campus, her eyes swollen from an hour of tears. "I am so stupid, so utterly stupid," she intoned in a litany of self-depreciation. "I thought they were my friends, but all they wanted was my help on the exam and the keys to my car. When they got what they needed, they made a joke of me and left me alone, again."

Discernment is a fruitful mix of street smarts, common sense and intuition — grounded in experience. You can learn from every human encounter, gaining insight into others or your own self. Unmasking includes the wisdom of discernment to set appropriate boundaries.

Can I Trust You with My Heart?

William Barclay articulates a question we all could ask: "I wonder if there is anyone to whom I would open my heart?" It is the relentless question of unmasking.

The philosopher Seneca gave the answer: "If you wish to be loved, love." There is no other way. The journey begins in unmasking.

Several years ago a popular song asked the question in another way: "Can I trust you with my heart?" Can I take the risk and open myself to you without fear of being hurt? I'm afraid the answer is no—there will always be risk and the very real danger of pain. Proverbs 22:24-25 warns against the risks inherent in some friendships: "Make no friends with those given to anger, and do not associate with hotheads, or you may learn their ways and entangle yourself in a snare."

I turn to Nouwen once more for his wise caution:

Friendship and love cannot develop in the form of an anxious clinging to each other. They ask for gentle fearless space in which we can move to and from each other. As long as our loneliness brings us together with the hope that together we no longer will be alone, we castigate each other with our unfulfilled and unrealistic desires for oneness, inner tranquility and the uninterrupted experience of communion.[5]

What is required then is that we offer hospitality, which begins with the act and art of unmasking. Here's the good news: hospitality is a skill that can be learned by all, though it is also an art that comes more naturally to some. As we practice this ancient art of hospitality, we create the possibility of standing together on the holy ground of friendship. Host and guest can remain as impersonal as a hotel manager with the one-hundredth guest of the night—polite and helpful but not offering true hospitality or they can learn to unmask and welcome the other in.

What are some "exercises" that will help me learn the skill of the hospitality of unmasking?

1. Practice good listening skills (see chapter four). Show interest in the other, give feedback and work hard to give the other person your complete attention. You can't just ask questions and then begin to talk about yourself. Wait for an answer. Listen for deep meanings and always ask yourself, *What have I learned about this person from our conversation? What do I know now that I didn't know previously?*

2. Practice asking good questions, relational questions that will draw out the other person to talk about feelings, inner issues and

personal concerns. Instead of "What line of work are you in?" ask, "What energizes you in your work life?" Or, "How are you different in your profession from the way you were a year ago?" There is a basic principle in the skill of conversation: we love to talk about ourselves. Learn to be a great host by asking great questions.

3. Don't practice "trivial pursuits" in conversation. Keep on guard against settling for superficial conversations and topics. Listen for twenty-four hours to your conversations. Keep a mental journal, noting your most repeated topics, themes and issues. Ask yourself, *Would I like to listen to a taped repeat of the day's conversations? Why or why not?*

4. Practice growth skills. Regularly ask yourself, *What can I do to improve my skills in asking questions? Whom do I know who asks great questions?*

5. Remember high-school chemistry. There is something magical about some friendships. Some friendships are like chemical reactions: they just happen. Some do not.

Hospitality is offered when I welcome you, risks and all, into a free and open space where we may learn to love each another. Not every new encounter will feel risky or open to excessive vulnerability, but every true friendship begins when I offer another person hospitality and welcome them into my world.

Study Questions

1. How would you finish the question "If you really knew me . . . "?

2. List your friendships according to the three levels described early in this chapter.

3. To whom have you been a Jonathan in your life?

4. Write a biography of the development of a recent friendship. How did it get started? What has helped it grow?

5. Are you a person of loyalty and commitment?

Three

My Door Is Always Open to You

Nobody sees a flower,
really—it is so small—we haven't
time, and to see takes time,
like to have a friend takes time.
GEORGIA O'KEEFE

Friendships grow through intentional choices for loyalty.

*T*HEY DREW A CIRCLE AND LEFT ME OUT." I READ THE phrase from Edwin Markham's poem and was instantly taken back to similar childhood moments of pain, rejection and sadness.

Can you at least identify with the feelings, if not the words? It is a power unlike any other, this power to exclude by closing the door. It is a lethal power, this power to refuse hospitality to another, the power to say "no" rather than "yes," "not now" rather than "today." It can be a harsh decision to reject rather than to welcome, and we each have our stories to tell of times when the circle has been drawn to keep us out.

Exclusion and rejection create deep scars and the potential for lifelong pain; in fact, the risks of intimacy and friendship carry in their hands a power unlike any other. If I reach out to you, you may choose to ignore me or, worse, reject me. If I dare to unmask for even a moment, the vulnerability of showing my true identity can set me up for one more heartbreak. If I trust you, even a little, you hold in your hands the power to hurt me. I know and suspect you know it too; we have all felt the pain of love's rejection. There is, however, no other way to friendship than through the doorway of taking risky choices which brings us to biblical perspective number two: *Friendships grow through intentional choices for loyalty.*

The book of Ruth tells the story of Naomi and her daughter-in-law Ruth. In Joyce Hollyday's book *Clothed with the Sun,* she characterizes the friendship of these two women as that of "vulnerable survivors." A famine in the region had caused Naomi to move from her own country to the land of Moab. Her husband and two sons died, leaving her alone in a foreign land with two foreign daughters-in-law. The future was bleak for this widow. Naomi was old and knew that she could not provide well for her family; thus she released the younger women to return to their families of origin, where they would receive care and protection. In a soliloquy she told them, "Turn back. It is not necessary for you to suffer just because God has dealt bitterly with me. You are young—you can remarry and lead a full life. If you continue with me there's no hope for marriage" (see Ruth 1:8-13).

A Case Study in Friendship

The story of Ruth and Naomi has been aptly called "a case study in friendship." It was a script for a friendship gone sour; it became instead the script of a friendship turned sweet.

Naomi's life had hit the wall of disaster, pain and suffering. One daughter-in-law turned back; the other, Ruth, refused to abandon Naomi and instead declared love and loyalty to her mother-in-law, her friend. Ruth said, "Do not press me to leave you or to turn back from following you! Where you go, I will go; Where you lodge, I will lodge; your people shall be my people, and your God my God" (Ruth 1:16).

In many weddings these words are used as a pledge of loyal commitment for husbands and wives, but we must remember their original context as words of loyalty from friend to friend, woman to woman. Genuine friendship can be demanding; love is not only for the easy times of sunshine and laughter but also for the rainy days of stress and struggle. Life confronts every friendship with challenges to loyalty. True friendships grow out of innumerable small choices which add up to big loyalty.

Hollyday describes the principle in the story of Ruth and Naomi: "At the heart of their success was a deep love and devotion to each other, an unbreakable bond of sisterhood. When one suffered, both suffered. When one was blessed, both were blessed. . . . By faithfulness, the sorrow that Ruth and Naomi bore together was turned to joy—sorrow halved, joy doubled, as the old adage says of friendship."[1]

Someone once said, "A friend is the one who walks in when everyone else walks out." Loyalty is that kind of intentional choice in friendship which brings growth. There is *selflessness* in Ruth's love for her friend Naomi. She made a careful choice to continue in the friendship and to cultivate its growth. Many have written about the *selfishness* of people today, especially in the twentysomething generation and its harsh exclusiveness. My experience with college students and recent graduates would challenge that viewpoint. We all fight the battle with our own selfishness, but I also see an intense hunger for friendships like that of Ruth and Naomi and the willingness of many to make the choices necessary for it.

The Hard Work of Love
Sentimentally I would like to believe that friendship unfolds in a natural, spontaneous way, without effort or intention; reality

argues strenuously against that naiveté. It may happen that way for some, but I think it is a rare exception. The choice to be loyal to a friend is oxygen given or withheld. To say yes breathes life into a relationship; to say no leads to eventual death. We choose to say yes or no in dozens or even hundreds of small, everyday choices. Do I call or not? Write or not? Visit or not? To choose another as friend is to say yes to two of life's most precious assets: time and place. I will spend time with you *here* in the real world of my busy life. I will spend time with you *now* in the real world of my busy life. It means I give you space in my schedule and create a place for us to be.

Sometimes you read words that ring true in a way that somehow won't let you go. The first time I read these words from M. Scott Peck, I had that experience.

Love is an act of will—namely, both an intention and an action. Will also implies choice. We do not have to love. We choose to love. . . . Love is not simply giving; it is *judicious* giving and judicious withholding as well. It is judicious praising and judicious criticizing. It is judicious arguing, struggling, confronting, urging, pushing and pulling in addition to comforting. It is leadership. The word "judicious" means requiring judgment, and judgment requires more than instinct; it requires thoughtful and often painful decision-making.[2]

Intentional choices then are the order of the day in the nurture of friendships. Though not always conscious, they are intended and chosen every time I create hospitality for you, every time I create a space of safety and welcome for you. What we were *not* told as children is what we all discovered on our own: learning the skill of friend making is hard.

Ecclesiastes 4:9-12 considers it worth the difficulty:

Two are better than one,
    because they have a good return for their work:
If one falls down,

his friend can help him up.
But pity the man who falls
   and has no one to help him up!
Also, if two lie down together, they will keep warm.
   But how can one keep warm alone?
Though one may be overpowered,
   two can defend themselves.
A cord of three strands is not quickly broken. (NIV)

Sharon might as well have been born on Saturn, she was so different from me. She dyed her hair purple twenty-five years before it was fashionable. She was poor, rough-hewn, out of sync, loud and avoided by everyone except her tiny circle of odd friends, and she sat next to me in junior-high homeroom and English. She was a social nonconformist in a culture that thrived on social conformity. Did she not notice or not care that she was different? I never knew. All I can tell you is that she stood out at precisely the moment I most wanted to fit in, but there she sat, next to me, day after day.

Perhaps I was worn down by the battering ram of familiarity—I saw her for two hours, five days a week! Perhaps it was just thirteen-year-old male hormones—she was a girl, after all, maybe even pretty behind the mask of a dissident's clothing, makeup and hairstyle. Or maybe *she* felt sorry for me that I was so incurably infected by a desperate longing to fit in. But it happened and I couldn't avoid it—she spoke to me!

She asked a question, followed, it seemed, by a hundred more. Once the first drop penetrated the dam, it burst and she seemed ruthlessly intent on getting me to talk. Behind me Richard watched the drama with intense interest, moving his chair noisily to alert me that the moment would not go unrecorded.

It was a moment of confrontation. There was an unwritten social code that proclaimed, "Clean-cut members of the button-down, churchgoing culture do not talk to Sharon or her kind."

Her friends drove fast cars, smoked in the school parking lot, openly swore while they talked about last night's party across town.

Now I won't tell you that I measured discerningly or wisely the action I was about to take, but it was impossible to miss the weighty significance of the moment. It was a watershed. Weakened by my own loneliness or driven by my own stunned curiosity, I made a conscious decision that day—I answered her question. I broke the social rules and talked to Sharon in public! In that moment of choice we crossed an invisible line into friendship.

By lunch that day Richard had made sure everyone knew that I had broken the social code, but it didn't matter. I had made my decision, and Sharon and I remained friends until the day she moved away.

Not every choice is as weighty as my break with junior-high conformity, but there are frequent decisions faced by all—for or against friendship. We may choose the act of loyalty and friendship or not. *Friendships grow through intentional choices for loyalty.*

Locking Hearts

Stu Weber writes about "God's design for masculine friendships" in a book entitled *Locking Arms.* The title is his metaphor for the loyalty of two men who stand shoulder to shoulder, man to man, against whatever life will bring. Although it's a descriptive phrase, especially for male friendships, I prefer another that it evokes in me: locking *hearts.* By our everyday choices we decide to lock hearts in loyal commitment to one another. Life is difficult enough; to face it alone is excruciating. Locking hearts begins when we choose to love another and continues as we confirm that love in numerous acts of loyalty.

Author and Christian activist John Perkins spoke on our campus and made a comment that struck me with great force. His life has influenced the life of the church in significant ways through his principles of racial reconciliation and strategies for incarnational ministry. Insightfully, Perkins said, "I could not do the work I do had it not been for the friends God has given me."

This man whose life has been such a beacon for justice and the gospel of Christ acknowledged his dependence on friendship—locking arms with partners in the cause of racial reconciliation and locking hearts in the work of ministry. Friendships grow through choices for loyalty. We stand strongest against the pressures of the battle when loyal friends stand alongside us.

We need the intimacy of friendships for many reasons:
- [ ] help when we fall
- [ ] the warmth of shared trust
- [ ] strength in times of trouble
- [ ] protection against life's assaults
- [ ] encouragement
- [ ] acceptance
- [ ] growth
- [ ] fun and laughter

Throughout his letters Paul talks about *koinōnia,* which means "to work together in the same direction, to share the load of life together, to build something in common." This is another important understanding of friendship: friendship grows most "naturally" in the soil of the choice to work together for common goals. C. S. Lewis writes,

> That is why those pathetic people who simply "want friends" can never make any. The very condition of having Friends is that we should want something else besides Friends. Where the truthful answer to the question *Do you see the same truth?* would be "I see nothing and I don't care about the truth; I only want a Friend," no Friendship can arise—though Affection of course may. There would be nothing for the Friendship to be *about;* and Friendship must be about something, even if it were

only an enthusiasm for dominoes or white mice. Those who have nothing can share nothing; those who are going nowhere can have no fellow-travelers."[3]

The Need for Belonging

Our need for belonging may drive us to find friends and seek to make others our friends, but there must be more that holds it together. I remember when I discovered this truth in my own young life at age ten. I was given a choice between piano lessons and Little League baseball and, of course, chose baseball. The world may have lost a musical genius, but I was not only choosing between being indoors and outdoors in the summer and between what I then considered a "sissy thing" and a macho thing. It was also a choice for belonging.

I became part of something; I belonged to a team. I had a shared identity with fifteen other boys gathered around what we perceived to be the important goal of playing baseball. One of the greatest days of my life was the day they passed out the team shirts and hats. My identity was secure: I was now a Glen Ellyn Mustang! The green hat with the huge white *G* rarely left my head during that summer in which we played truly awful baseball. We lost far more than we won, and I struck out far more than I hit, but it did not matter because I was part of something important, something greater than myself.

Friendship is about belonging—that's why friendships grow through intentional choices and why loyalty is so important. Just as in a healthy marriage, good friends must decide again and again to belong.

In the movie *Skylark*—a sequel to the novel and movie *Sarah, Plain and Tall*—we are told the story of a turn-of-the-century pioneer woman who leaves the lush beauty and green forests of coastal Maine to travel to the isolated wheat fields of Kansas as a mail-order bride. In time a deadly drought creates a dust bowl, and many families abandon their homes, farms and fields in desperation and failure. Sarah struggles with the land and its grip on her husband. His love for the land is as deep as her love for the sea, whose absence she mourns. Deep within, she feels that she just doesn't belong to the land. She cannot understand why her husband loves it. She doesn't know what he sees in the ungiving and unforgiving earth, so dry, barren and wasted from the drought.

In time, however, she begins to fall deeply in love with her husband and his children and resists his decision to send her back to Maine to her family. He convinces her that it is the only way they will survive, so she travels east with the children and is gone for many long months. Now she is home again, where she "belongs," near the Atlantic in a land that is green, lush and fertile. Meanwhile the drought continues, and her separation from her husband causes her new loneliness and pain.

When the rains finally come and crops are profitable, he travels to Maine to take her back to Kansas. She now faces the greatest decision of her life: to stay where she "belongs" in the green beauty of Maine or to return to the farm. She makes her decision and departs for the farmlands of Kansas.

What moved me most was the final scene: Sarah steps onto the farm with a stick in her hand. In a profoundly symbolic gesture she displays her decision for all to see. With that stick she writes a single word in the soil—her name, Sarah. She has learned to see through the eyes of another and to love with her own heart. In the end she chooses to belong to something greater than her own identity. In that act of belonging she declares her loyalty to the land and her new home.

Poet Kathleen Norris had a similar experience when she moved from New York City to the Dakotas to sell the family farm. To her surprise she has stayed there for more than twenty years and learned something essential: "not only to know where you are but also to love what you find there."[4]

It is a lesson that applies to friendship as well. Often we operate with the mentality of "consumer friendships," approaching people with our personal list of tastes, preferences and inclinations. If our friends turn out to be different from our tastes, do we replace them as quickly as we might change a pair of socks because they are the wrong style or color? For a host the task is a singular one: to welcome the guest, to receive the guest, to accept the guest *as she is*.

The Discovery of Friendship

Many people think of friendship as the goal or the product and "go after friends." We try to "make friends" when perhaps friends are better *discovered* through the process of living life. Dietrich Bonhoeffer believed this to be true in the development of the friendship of a community. Christians try very hard to build community or fellowship rather than to discover it. He reminds us that God has been at work in bringing us fellowship before we were. "Because God has already laid the only foundation of our fellowship, because God has bound us together in one body with other Christians in Jesus Christ, long before we entered into common life with them, we enter into common life not as demanders but as thankful recipients." I don't think that means we are to wait passively for others to always take the initiative, but we need to discover rather than force friendships. If a relationship is to mature, a naturalness must develop.

One woman said that "it is also important to remember . . . that we as Christians are to build up the body of Christ, and that body includes more than two people. We need to cultivate friendships with other women as part of our share in building up the fellowship, not merely as an insurance policy against loneliness." In other words, we need to remember that friendship is very often a byproduct of doing something else, something valuable and compelling.

Sometimes we may bypass friendship because we're looking for the wrong thing! Instead of being on the lookout for someone with whom to create friendship, we might find friendship more often if we're on the lookout for something of value and importance *to do* with our lives. The unexpected surprise for many people is that they discover friendships *along the way* as they are busily involved in other things. Students who are involved in team sports, music ensembles, drama troupes or other group projects understand this very well; friendships often grow out of the shared activity itself.

Every fall I attend a banquet sponsored by our college football team. I watch as students stand to talk about their experience as members of the team. The first year I went I expected to hear a lot of conversation about yardage, passes caught, points scored and other statistics. Instead I heard about friendships that had grown during the long season of competitive football. Men stood with tears in their eyes to thank other men for rich friendships that "just happened" as they spent hours in practice and games together. I no longer expect to hear statistics; now I go to watch husky, strong men talk with emotion and tenderness about friendship that comes as a byproduct of pursuing a shared goal.

As I look back on the recent years of my life, I identify three clusters of friends with whom I discovered the hospitality of good friendships. Paul was a fellow pastor in Washington State who took the step of vulnerability with me and invited himself to meet with me on a consistent basis. I wasn't sure about this idea in the beginning stages, but he persisted, and for six years we met approximately every two weeks to "lock arms" in shared life and ministry.

When I left Washington, I took the initiative in a new place with several men and invited them to do what Paul and I had done. For nearly six years a group of men sat in the corner of the 26th Street Market in Sioux Falls, locking hearts in friendship, fellowship, companionship, prayer and accountability. For the past seven years I have done the same with two men, Steve and Jim, in separate informal times of shared commitment.

What I have shared with all these men over the years has been what I believe is the discovery of the gift we are to each other. We don't feel the need to change the others through strategies of modification; instead we decide to accept and love each other as we are.

Hospitality, therefore, means primarily the creation of a free space where the stranger can enter and become a friend instead of an enemy. Hospitality is not to change people, but to offer them space where change can take place. . . . The paradox of hospitality is that it wants to create emptiness, not a fearful emptiness, but a friendly emptiness where strangers can enter and discover themselves as created free: free to sing their own songs, speak their own languages, dance their own dances; free also to leave and follow their own vocations. Hospitality is not a subtle invitation to adopt the life style of the host, but the gift of a chance for the guest to find his own.[5]

A student sat in my office with sadness in his heart and voice and said, "You know, Keith, I don't think I know a single person I could call at any hour of the day or night if I was in trouble." That is a cry of loneliness that reflects isolation and protectiveness. I grieve for that student and long for him to gain a biblical perspective: *friendships are maintained only through intentional acts of loyalty and a heart of commitment to your friend.* Many of us wait for the other to show us loyalty when, in fact, it is a step we both must take. Why? Because life brings us pain! Every one of us faces struggles, battles, crises and trauma at one time or another.

The power in this principle is that friendships grow precisely in the heat of the battle. It is when the going gets tough that friendships can grow the most. We can learn from Ruth and Naomi, who reached out to each other in the midst of their troubles. Adversity offered them choices to be made for or against loyalty: they chose the loyalty of friendship. They acted to care for one another in intentional acts of loyal friendship.

Not everyone does. That's why we all carry scars from childhood friends who chose to belong to others and left us behind.

Think back to a childhood experience of belonging—a team, club, orchestra or group. What made it important to you? Now think about a time in which a friend "replaced" you in order to belong to others. Have there been other friends whose relationship has been constant and loyal? What do these experiences teach you about belonging, loyalty and yourself?

When I Carry Your Load

Galatians 6 contains two contrasting images that are pertinent to this principle. Paul tells us in verse 2 that we are to carry one another's burdens and turns around in verse 5 to say "all must carry their own loads." Isn't that a direct contradiction? What did he mean?

The imagery from an army on the march is captivating. The burdens described in verse 2 are those loads too heavy for someone to carry alone—the group's tent, food, ropes and other equipment. Verse 5 refers to the individual pack, the load that is an individual's personal responsibility. Some things we must carry alone. Friendships will not mature when one person demands that others carry the backpack of personal responsibility. Loyalty does not mean I do for you what you are able to do for yourself; it refers instead to helping carry the heavy loads you are not able to carry alone.

I picked up mail today and read about a "risk-free" trial offer. There is no such offer in friendships. If you build a friendship in order to guard against your own loneliness, it may work for a while but you may be replaced and left with your own familiar loneliness. There are no guarantees in friendship. Sometimes your friendships change.

A friend said to me recently, "It's very difficult to celebrate my best friend's engagement when I haven't had a date in six months."

Another friend said, "Peter and I were like blood brothers in high school. We went to college together and eventually lived in the same fraternity as roommates and fraternity brothers. We shared our lives to the deepest parts we had. We learned to go deep when his brother died followed soon after by the death of my father. Sure, we needed alcohol to break down the walls and help us go deep, but at least we had something real we could hold on to. In time he married and moved to another part of the country. I spent a week with him in Phoenix recently, the worst week of my life. We lived not only in different parts of the country but, as far as values and priorities, in different worlds. Whatever we once had was gone. It was the most superficial and shallow week I've ever spent."

There is pain and there are seasons to friendships, what the writer of Ecclesiastes called "times." We'll talk about those seasons in chapter five. There are certainly no formulas for friendship that work with universal success, because relationships tap into deep and sometimes painful parts of our history, psyche and dysfunctions. Unhealthy people are sometimes not ideal candidates for healthy friendships. Selfish people are sometimes not ideal candidates for generous friendships. We need to be aware of the difficulties in all our relationships.

You can choose to avoid people, but more helpfully you can learn to understand them and assist in their growth. Friendships grow as we continue to love; love is expressed through acceptance and loyalty.

Will any of that *guarantee* friendship? No, we need to get rid of the fantasy that we can guarantee anything in relationships. There are not "six easy steps" to healthy and happy friendships. That thinking may sell a lot of books or magazines, but there are no guarantees in relationships.

The words of C. S. Lewis cannot be read too many times:

But, for the Christian, there are, strictly speaking, no chances. A secret Master of the Ceremonies has been at work. Christ, who said to the disciples, "Ye have not chosen me, but I have chosen you," can truly say to every group of Christian friends "You have not chosen one another but I have chosen you for one another." The Friendship is not a reward for our discrimination and good taste in finding one another out. It is the instrument by which God reveals to each the beauties of all the others. They are no greater than the beauties of a thousand other men; by Friendship God opens our eyes to them. They are, like all beauties derived from Him, and then, in a good Friendship, increased by Him through the Friendship itself, so that it is His instrument for creating as well as for revealing.[6]

Ruth offered Naomi a hospitality of the heart that altered the course of her personal history. Her open door to her mother-in-law and friend did not come without cost, and it required a lifetime of intentional choices. Still, I never get the impression that it mattered to Naomi. When it came to Ruth, her door was always open.

Study Questions

1. Are you more like Ruth or Naomi in your friendships?

2. How do you respond to the quote from M. Scott Peck in this chapter?

3. What does "belonging" mean to you? How do you seek it in your relationships?

4. With whom do you "lock hearts"? Do you have a group of deeply trusted friends?

5. Discuss the idea that friendship is the byproduct of doing something else valuable or compelling. Do you agree? Why or why not?

Four

"Somebody Nobody Knows"

No one can find a full life without feeling
understood by at least one person.
PAUL TOURNIER

A friend learns how to listen.

*E*RIC AND I TALKED FOR THE FIRST TIME IN MY OFFICE ONE
afternoon. He had a thinly disguised excuse for meeting me, but
the disguise soon dropped away. He blurted out the real reason
for his visit: "This may sound crazy to you because people think
I have it all together, but I am dying of loneliness. I walk through
the day past hundreds of people and talk to many, but I don't
believe my life matters to anyone at all."

His words reminded me of an old sixties song that repeated the
words "somebody nobody knows." Loneliness is not unique; it is
something we have all experienced. Cited as one of the greatest
causes of suicide today, it certainly contributes to much emotional
pain. It is a common feeling and a devastating way to live. I
describe it as a deep ache of being alone and lonely, of feeling
unimportant. The feeling that no one would know or care if you
come or you go, the feeling that you are invisible. You live in a

place where people crowd around and bump into you, jostle you on their way to somewhere else, on their way to something important. Can you identify with this deep, deep hurt, this feeling that you are passed by?

It Is Not Good . . .

In Genesis 2, verses 18-20 set up the problem. Verse 18 shows God evaluating the young creation, and for the first time in the entire creation narrative, God says something is "*not* good." "It is not good that the man should be alone. I will make him a helper as his partner."

Why did the man need a helper? Because he was not complete in himself. Why did God declare that it was not good for him to be alone? Because no man is complete in himself. No woman is complete in herself. Humankind was created for relationship, and a satisfying relationship had not yet been found. The man was lonely, and there was, as yet, no one to know him and help him deal with those feelings.

Please do not misunderstand me. I am not equating singleness with Adam's aloneness. Singleness is not a second-best choice for people; for some, in fact, it is a spiritual gift from the hand of the Creator. The aloneness and loneliness of Adam, however, was an ontological sense of disconnection from any other who might be a companion.

In verse 19 we see that God began to work on the problem. He brought the animals to Adam to see what he would name them — in effect, to learn about them and become acquainted with them. Adam needed to spend time with them so he could study them and name them appropriately, but even that work and relationship didn't fill the incompleteness in the man. The image of God in humankind is that we are created as spiritual beings with a capacity for companionship. When we are without friends or companions, we are lonely.

Loneliness is a common and difficult problem to face. Many college students face the problem of loneliness most acutely *after* graduation as they move from the life of the herd to the life of the hermit. At least that's the way it feels to some. In May they had friends in the dorm, across the quad, in the Bible study group and all over the campus—too many friends to keep up with on a daily basis—but now it is June and they're in an apartment, living alone in a crowded city. *How can I make new friends? This is hard work. Where do you meet people, especially Christians?*

Others struggle with the "single person/married friends" syndrome, the struggle of being the one member of the group who isn't married. *How do I move ahead with friendships when all of my former roommates and best friends have moved ahead themselves with husbands or wives?*

Some live in a work world with older or younger colleagues whose life stages don't coincide with theirs. You are twenty-five, new on the job and the youngest member of the office. The rest are married or divorced, parents or grandparents. You live alone and are bored with the singles scene. *Are the bars or church single groups the only places to find friends?*

How then do you develop acquaintances who will possibly become new and close friends? Biblical perspective number three may sound like a simplistic answer; in fact, it may be the most practical of the seven biblical perspectives: *a friend learns how to listen.* The only door I know that opens into the heart of loneliness is the door of a listening ear.

Job was in trouble; Job was in pain. He grieved because of the overwhelming loss of job, family, wealth, status and authority. The story of Job is told with exaggerated intensity to make the point clear: Job was a hurting human being. But Job was not alone in his pain; he had friends who came to visit him in the midst of his grief, friends who knew him well and seemed to care deeply for him. They did not leave him to suffer alone. They did not want him to feel the loneliness of painful grief. They arrived at his side to help poor old Job, but look at the "help" they offered their suffering friend:

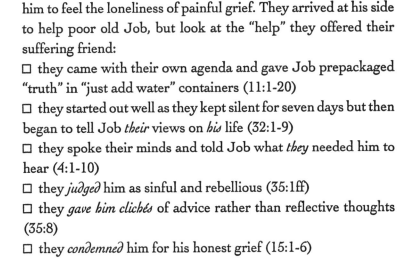

☐ they came with their own agenda and gave Job prepackaged "truth" in "just add water" containers (11:1-20)

☐ they started out well as they kept silent for seven days but then began to tell Job *their* views on *his* life (32:1-9)

☐ they spoke their minds and told Job what *they* needed him to hear (4:1-10)

☐ they *judged* him as sinful and rebellious (35:1ff)

☐ they *gave him clichés* of advice rather than reflective thoughts (35:8)

☐ they *condemned* him for his honest grief (15:1-6)

What We Need Most

Job's friends came to him with their own agenda and broke the primary law of good friendship: a friend knows how to listen. Maybe it is more honest to say a friend *learns* how to listen.

What do people need most from a friend? That's not hard to figure. Ask yourself, *What do I need most from my friends? Do I need their ideas, viewpoints, opinions and thoughts? Do I need their interpretation of my life and its problems? Or, more than anything else, do I need them to listen to me?* What we long for most deeply is acceptance, honesty, encouragement and a listening ear. *Friends learn how to listen.*

A listening ear is one of the greatest powers that exists in the universe. When I listen I honor you. When I listen I accept you as you are. When I listen I validate both your words and your thoughts. A listening friendship creates a hospitable place for another person. In that hospitality I create a free and friendly space where you can feel safe and welcome.

In the NIV translation of Romans 15:7 we read, "Accept one another, then, just as Christ accepted you." The NRSV uses the language of hospitality: "Welcome one another, therefore, just as Christ has welcomed for you, for the glory of God." One writer said, "This is the bedrock of friendship, the living core of any relationship. A-c-c-e-p-t-a-n-c-e. Come as you are. I like you. I love you. I will do anything for you. And nothing you could ever do could turn me away from you."[1] That kind of listening is more than merely polite hospitality.

How does listening like that happen? How does it work? Don't all of us know how to listen well? Absolutely not! Listening is an art that has faded in our world of constant noise and stimulation. Words are broadcast endlessly. We are barraged by the demand for listening everywhere we go.

I sat at dinner tonight with my family at a popular restaurant. We were there, in part, to celebrate a graduation and to spend time with one another over a good meal. Instead we ignored one another because of the distraction of television screens in every corner of the restaurant. From every direction came the blare of words and more words.

Distracting noise is everywhere, accomplishing untold damage done to relationships. "Listen to me!" is a demanding plea, everywhere we go. Mary Rose O'Reilly writes,

> Modern life with its din of canned music and commercial entreaty, its appeals and drives, its reviews and performance evaluations, trains us not to attend but to tune out. There is much to hear, but little worth listening to. In an environment of overstimulation, the commitment to spend time simply listening constitutes a radical experiment in friendship.[2]

Listening Is Radical!

You probably have had times when you were certain that no one in the world was listening to you. I have. What we need is not merely someone who listens in a physical sense; rather, we need to be heard. We need to know that what we say isn't being interpreted prematurely but that we are allowed to name the truth as we see it.

Stephen R. Covey agrees with that and even defines one of his "seven habits of highly effective people" as *empathic communication:* "Seek first to understand, then to be understood."

When another person speaks, we're usually "listening" at one of four levels. We may be *ignoring* another person, not really listening at all. We may practice *pretending.* "Yeah. Uh-huh. Right." We may practice *selective listening,* hearing only certain parts of the conversation. . . . Or we may even practice *attentive listening,* paying attention and focusing energy on the words that are being said. But very few of us ever practice the fifth level, the highest form of listening, *empathic listening.*[3]

Empathic listening means that I attempt to listen so well that I get inside your mind and see what you see. I empty myself of my preconceptions of how it is for you and let your words paint the inner landscape for me. The colors from your palette will create the tones and hues that I will learn to see.

Empathic listening fulfills the ultimate purpose of communication, the transfer of meaning between two people. It is one of the essential steps to friendships that run deep. Does it "solve" the "problem" of loneliness or resolve the pain of rejection? I can only say that it opens a door to such healing.

Bruce Larson wrote a book years ago entitled *No Longer Strangers,* in which he quoted a poem written by his son Peter, who was then fourteen years old. It is a plaintive cry for the kind of listening I'm writing about.

Hello out there, world;
It's me in here.
Can't you see me?
What? You're having trouble hearing me?

But I'm in here.
Yes, that's right.
Inside where?
Inside myself, of course.

The outside shell is very thick;
I'm having trouble getting out.
Who am I? You say I don't sound like myself?
That's because you've never heard me.

This other guy? Oh, he's the shell I told you about.
You say that's me?
No, I'm in here;
He's just my protection.

Protection from what?
From you, the world.
I can't be hurt here.
You see, my shell keeps you away.

You, the world, are pain.
I'm safe in here;
I will never be laughed at.
The shell? Oh, he doesn't mind laughter.
Come to think of it,
I'm comfortable in here.
Why should I leave?
Hello, world, still listening?

What's that, world?
I thought for a minute you said something.
It was a faint voice;
It sounded human, real, I thought.

I thought it was answering me.

Maybe not.
I can't hear too well inside this shell.
Well, I feel funny, sleepy,
And it's so comfortable in here, world.[4]

Listening to another person is a sacred act by which we offer a safe and welcome place often in the midst of such fear and pain. Peter's words are so powerful precisely because he is ambiguous about his need. He knows he wants to be heard but has discovered that it may be unsafe to be heard and rejected. The listening ear of a good friend is a means of creating the safety needed for our emotional and psychological well-being.

How do we listen to another? Listening is prayerfully, carefully, receptively attending to the truth you show me. Effective listening involves both *skills* and *attitude*.

Basic Skills

Any introductory communications course teaches certain skills for listening.

☐ Listening requires concentration.

☐ Listening requires feedback, which shows that you understand what is being said.

☐ Listening is the skill of following or tracking with the ideas, feelings and content of the other.

☐ Listening begins with the skill of "joining," in which I connect with you, your topic and your meanings.

☐ Listening seeks to understand—communication is essentially the transfer of meaning.

☐ Listening ears are helped by focused eyes. In the Western world good eye contact is evidence of good listening.

☐ Listening is an active part of good hospitality.

Basic Attitude

Those skills can be learned, but they are dependent on the attitude of hospitality, in which I willingly invite you in and welcome you as my guest. Using listening *skills* without an *attitude* of genuine interest in the other is simply a gross form of manipulation. Listening is an authentic act of hospitality in which I willingly invite you in.

Differences fade in importance as two people—like branches of a river—meet and join together in the flow of friendship. Instead of a violent collision there can be a harmonious union of distinct and divergent lives. Two stories become one as two people find each other and discover that despite the differences, friendship is the common story line.

I suppose Ron and I were about as different as any two human beings could be. He was a high-school dropout, a blue-collar plywood mill worker, while I was a college- and seminary-educated professional, a pastor. As a young man Ron was offered two options: join the army or go back to the juvenile detention system in the state of Oregon. I was a "good" kid, a law-abiding citizen. He went to the deltas of Vietnam at precisely the same time I was on the college campus, raising questions and struggling with the politics of the war in Southeast Asia. Ron was a rough-and-tumble man in manner and language; I had lived in the shadow of the church.

The woman Ron wanted to marry, Cheryl, lived down the street from our home in Tacoma, Washington, where I pastored a small inner-city church. Our early conversations weren't promising. I wasn't impressed, and neither was he. His honesty kept him away from churches where questions weren't allowed or where hypocrisy might hide. Ron hadn't been to church for many long months but had a hunger to know truth. He was also in love and ready to do whatever it would take to get this young preacher to perform the wedding.

I cannot tell you just how it happened, but I can tell you that as the days turned into weeks and months turned into years we lived as neighbors and became brothers. We shared a love for camping, but even there our differences showed: he arrived with a motor home filled with electric utensils and enough food for a regiment of soldiers, while my family slept in a tent from Sears. We met for a time at 6:00 a.m. three days a week to condition ourselves for a Mount Rainier climb and ran our five miles together in trustful conversation. The running wasn't much of a draw, and the early-morning schedule wasn't much of a motivator, but the coffee and talk on Ron's porch after the run were enough to get us up and going (most of the time).

I performed Ron's wedding, baptized him and Cheryl, baptized two of his daughters and buried Cheryl's grandmother. We had a serious snowball fight the one day it snowed during our years in Tacoma and spent hours and hours in laughter over kielbasa and pinochle. Our kids lived in each other's yards and living rooms as much as in their own. Through diapers and trikes, karate and bikes, paper routes and scouting, our lives were intermingled.

Late one night Cheryl called me to tell me there had been an accident at the mill. One of Ron's workers stood on the assembly line to free a jammed saw just as the line lurched into operation and caused him to fall. Parts of both feet had been cut off. I didn't know the worker, but I did know Ron, so I raced to the hospital to be with him. Ron was there with the worker's wife and led her in a prayer for her husband with the most honest words of faith I have ever heard. He was excited but not agitated. There was a calm about him that surprised me.

Later we went to Ron's house, and I watched him slowly unwrap his emotions. The violence of the accident, combined with the blood at the scene, took him back to the rice paddies of Vietnam and the many friends he had watched die. We shared a long and painful night together. He told me the story of how he won his military medal and the scars he carries to this very day.

A couple of years later I prepared to move from the neighborhood to another state. Ron was there for the final party at my house but seemed restless and distant. He gave me a gift that had personal significance to us and then privately handed me another, smaller package. He grabbed me around the shoulders, said "I love you, brother," and walked out of the house with tears running down his face. When my own tears slowed down I opened the package, and my heart nearly stopped beating. I held in my hand his medal from Vietnam.

Paul said, "Be devoted to one another in brotherly love" (Rom 12:10 NIV). Love begins with listening and is shown through listening. Paul also said that love isn't possessive (1 Cor 13:4), which means that listening is a two-way street.

Over the years, I listened to Ron's many questions as a pastor-professional and tried to give theological truth to him. In time that was transformed into mutual times of musing and wondering as I listened to his continuing questions and he to mine. We weren't always looking for answers; it was enough to ask good questions. We weren't always able to agree with one another; it was enough to hear each other. He listened to my dreams and ideas for the future and I to his. Our lives were intertwined around shared hours—and listening.

How to Ruin a Friendship

I nearly titled this chapter "How to Ruin a Friendship" because friendships are destroyed by the relationship sins of possessiveness, selfishness and the refusal to listen. Job's friends were guilty of them all. They knew how to interpret Job's life for him and did that freely and with great conviction.

Job's friends came to Job with a grand motivation: to help

their friend in a time of great distress and grief. They listened for the traditional period of mourning but then turned off their ears and turned on their mouths.

Job was the one who did the listening—until he could stand it no longer and raged at them in disappointment and anger.

Look, my eye has seen all this,
my ear has heard and understood it.
What you know, I also know;
I am not inferior to you.
But I would speak to the Almighty,
and I desire to argue my case with God.
As for you, you whitewash with lies;
all of you are worthless physicians.
If you would only keep silent,
that would be your wisdom! (Job 13:1-5)

Later he said, "Let me have silence, and I will speak" (13:13). Job's cry is the cry of Western society and culture today: "All I really want is for someone to listen, the chance to make my case, the opportunity to be heard!" The outrageous behaviors all around us are voices begging for friends who will listen. Douglas Steere writes, "To 'listen' another's soul into a condition of disclosure and discovery may be almost the greatest service that any human being ever performs for another."[5]

How can you ruin a friendship?

☐ Don't listen.

☐ Get possessive with a friend's time.

☐ Be jealous and demand more and more while you give less and less.

☐ Learn to fake your true feelings and to disguise your emotions.

☐ Be a phony; don't reveal your true self.

☐ Don't reciprocate the "unmasking" that another initiates. The unbalanced relationship where only one becomes vulnerable will not last long.

Dialogue Between Two Somebodies

When you listen to me you free my heart and allow me entry to your heart as well. We learn to share the road together, the road that will lead us to the very heart of God.

Glenn Kehrein and Raleigh Washington have publicly declared themselves to be best friends on such a road. For more than a decade they have worked together in the tough neighborhood of Austin in Chicago. Glenn is Caucasian and Raleigh African-American. They share ministry at Rock Church and Circle Urban Ministries. They work together every day. They live a life of high visibility, high demands and certainly high stress. Everything seems to be stacked against the success of their work and relationship—racial issues, economic struggles, expectations and life itself.

What keeps them on track and able to maintain a friendship in a world that is increasingly racist? They talk about the principle of intentionality in their book *Breaking Down Walls: A Model for Reconciliation in an Age of Racial Strife.* Recently I heard them describe their strategy for good listening. Once a month they go to a pancake house for a morning of conversation. Their schedules are cleared so they are not disturbed by interruptions of other "important" or "urgent" business. They meet to clear the air and tell each other the truth. They meet to put their hurts and frustrations on the table so they can walk back into the "hood," arms locked and walking in step together. They trust each other enough to listen and to hear. I have heard them say numerous times that the key to their friendship is honesty and listening ears.

Listening to another tell the truth may be the essence of hospitality. I invite you into my world not with exploitation or competition but with receptivity and welcome. In our conversations the "somebody nobody knows" becomes a "somebody greatly loved." As Henri Nouwen expresses it,

To be receptive to the stranger in no way implies that we have to become neutral "nobodies." Real receptivity asks for confrontation because space can only be a welcoming space when there are clear boundaries, and boundaries are limits between which we define our own position. . . . An empty house is not a hospitable house. . . . When we want to be really hospitable we not only have to receive strangers but also to confront them by an unambiguous presence, not hiding ourselves behind neutrality but showing our ideas, opinions and life style clearly and distinctly. No real dialogue is possible between somebody and a nobody.[6]

Study Questions

1. Rate your listening skills on a scale from 1 to 10 (10 = excellent).

2. Ask three friends to rate your listening skills on the same scale. Compare the ratings you gave and received.

3. Recall a time when someone you love truly listened to you. What made it memorable?

4. Recall the most recent time you asked someone to listen to something important and they "just went through the motions." Contrast how this felt in comparison to the feelings in question 3.

5. List three listening skills you know will improve your own listening abilities. Commit yourself to work on these in the coming weeks.

Five

The Seasons of Friendship

We go from threshold to threshold with something
pulling us forward and something pulling us back.
KEN GIRE

Friendships change and that's okay.
SCOTT PEARCY

There are seasons to friendship.

TIME IS AN ELUSIVE FACTOR IN RELATIONSHIPS. WHAT IS
time? How do you define this "invisible partner" in all relationships? Minutes pass in a chronological precision that is undeni-
able but we also know the deeper experience of time's movement
as fast or slow; it "flies" or "drags," "races" or "takes forever."

Wisely, the Greeks had different words for those different
experiences of time. *Chronos* means the simple passage of minutes,
hours, days and years. Chronological time is the sequence of life's
passage. A watch is accurately called a chronometer, an instrument by which we measure time's passing. *Kairos* means a moment
"pregnant" with meaning, densely significant, ripe with meaning,
thickly textured.

Just as there are "teachable moments" when our readiness for
learning is "timely," so there are "ready moments" in the "times"
of friends. Conversations can be as alive as a puppy set free to

romp in the garden or as bland as a bowl of leftover oatmeal. There are rich moments when people encounter each other in the animation of life that contains something more than the mere progression of minutes and hours.

Four of us sat in a coffee shop on the north side of Chicago. We were just passing time, enjoying an evening's break from an intense class. The coffee was good and the dessert was an attraction, but the conversation was the unexpected reward. I hope you've had times like that time was for us. We found common questions and the common ground of a spiritual quest that built instantaneous bridges of meaning between us. We spoke and were heard in a leisurely and welcoming exchange of stories. In a very short time we mined deep places in each other's histories and imagined deeper places yet in each other's futures. As the fireplace crackled its warmth into the room, the conversation became a container holding the warmth of grace for suspended moments of time richly shared.

Chronos moments merely pass; kairos moments are like a long, slow drink of water to a parched and thirsty traveler. Quickly gone but long remembered are the kairos moments when friends literally give time to one another, aware of its magic or meaning. As we finished our evening together, I remembered *where* we were and excitedly reminded my friends of the seemly collision of time and place—our evening was spent at a coffee shop called Uncommon Ground located on Grace Street.

Moments and hours in relationships gather together as seasons in time. The rare experience at Uncommon Ground traverses abruptly to the all-too-common ground located on the side streets of relationships-in-time. Not all friendship moments are like that uncommon evening of grace. Such moments are occasions for the celebration and grand appreciation of time. Still, I have come to understand that the ever-present but invisible dimension in every relationship is time. To comprehend the meaning of time in a relationship requires wise discernment. The writer of Ecclesiastes sang a poetic song, which reveals inspired truth in a series of memorable couplets.

For everything there is a season, and a time for every matter under heaven:
a time to be born, and a time to die;
a time to plant, and a time to pluck up what is planted;
a time to kill, and a time to heal;
a time to break down, and a time to build up;
a time to weep, and a time to laugh;
a time to mourn, and a time to dance;
a time to throw away stones, and a time to gather stones together;
a time to embrace, and a time to refrain from embracing;
a time to seek, and a time to lose;
a time to keep, and a time to throw away;
a time to tear, and a time to sew;
a time to keep silence, and a time to speak;
a time to love, and a time to hate;
a time for war, and a time for peace. (3:1-8)

The poet not only describes "real life," he invites us to participate in the kairos moments of time's richest events: birthing, planting, breaking down, weeping, mourning, throwing away, embracing, seeking, keeping, tearing, keeping silence, loving, warring; dying, harvesting, building, laughing, dancing, gathering, refraining, losing, throwing, sewing, speaking, hating and making peace. It is elegant poetry because it is human poetry written by one who has lived long enough to attend to the importance of time. There are seasons to life, he says, "times" which converge as seasons.

Our amassed experiences become embodied in the seasons of friendships. If friendships last long enough over time, there will be many seasons—perhaps all of the seasons the poet envisions "under heaven." Biblical perspective number four encourages us to see with a long-term outlook: *There are seasons to friendships.*

Friendships have seasons of fertility, seasons of growth and freshness but also seasons of decay, decline and stale monotony. There are seasons of storm, in which there is turbulence in the air, as well as seasons of sunshine and blue skies. Relationships cannot be measured by the accumulation of "minutes" as much as the experience of "moments"; not chronos time but kairos moments, all of which are gathered together into the reality of seasons. Friendships change over time, sometimes in the natural flow of our personal histories and transitions, sometimes because of crisis, hurt or anger. They can ebb like the low tide of the ocean and they can flow back in power at high tide. People change over time and friendships reflect that same dynamic quality. *There are seasons to friendships.*

Carmen and Linda became friends in elementary school. They were inseparable and lived in each other's lives as sisters. Their friendship was rich and deep, and seemed impervious to change, but the normal passage of time caused a natural parting of ways until they lost meaningful contact with each other for years. Recently they rediscovered each other and have returned to a friendship that began thirty-five years ago. Paula Ripple has helpfully envisioned the seasons of the earth as suggestive of the stages or "qualities of the seasons of friendship."

Spring is the time of the newness of friendship. "There is an excitement about the ease with which new friends share and discover together. . . . When relationships are new, the discovery process is wondrous and open. . . . New friendships seem easier to sustain because there has been no time of testing, no history of failure, no past memory of coldness or conflict. It is a time to notice the life that is there and growing. This season, is, therefore, a time of hope." . . .

Summer is the season of sunshine and growth. Like the summer after the spring planting time, it is a time of "let it be" and "let it grow." There is a sense of coming to feel at home with a friend no longer "new." . . .

Fall is a season of melancholy and transition. As the summer's warmth fades in preparation for the cold winter, this season in friendship is a time of loneliness. "Seldom do two friends grow in the same way and at the same rate. There is an insecurity in growing to a place new to me and yet unknown to my friend. . . ."

Winter is the season that may lack the color and vibrancy of fall and spring but is "filled with silentness" and memory. "It is a time of reflective quiet when friends experience the wisdom and rewards of having invested well in each of the other seasons."[1]

"Seasons" is the biblical poet's metaphor for the many transitions friendships encounter in time. In this chapter I want to reflect on this biblical insight: *There are seasons to friendship.*

Seasons of Beginnings

Friendships begin and end and may even begin again in fascinating and unpredictable ways. I was intrigued recently by applying Jesus' teachings about the four seeds to four types of friendships I have known. In Matthew's Gospel, Jesus talks about the fate of several seeds after they were handled by a farmer.

☐ Some fell on the pathway, and birds came and ate it up.

☐ Some fell on rocky places, where it sprang up quickly but died when the sun came out because of the shallow soil.

☐ Some fell among thorns and grew up quickly but was choked quickly as the thorns grew alongside it.

☐ Some fell on good soil, where it was nurtured, tended and produced a great harvest (Mt 13:1-9).

Curiously, my friendships have been like the experience of those four seeds.

☐ Some relationships were chance encounters, "on the pathway," that never really got started. The potential was there, and the possibility for a friendship existed, but it never grew past a casual encounter. Other things came along and ate up the possibility of the friendship.

☐ Some relationships sprang up quickly and held great promise for much, much more but were never given the proper care needed for a relationship to mature, deepen and grow. They remained shallow, and the promise died just as abruptly as it was born. Or they came at rough times when I was just too hardened by circumstances to welcome something new, when my outer shell was brittle and resistant to a new possibility.

☐ Some friendships grew quickly but were choked out by thorny distractions of what I call "too muchism." Too much to do, too much to work on, too much to think about, too much happening to give the relationship the time and care it needed. The thorns were sometimes very good and important things that simply choked out my time or energy. They distracted me from what could have become productive and fruitful relationships.

☐ And some few relationships found their way into deep, fertile soil where they were cared for, fed and watered and out of which have emerged harvests of thirty, sixty or a hundred times what was planted. These are relationships that have been weeded and maintained over many "growing seasons" and out of which have come lifelong friendships of the highest quality.

Seasons of Growth

I sat at Davanni's with a group of friends sharing a pizza and an evening of valuable conversation. "I just had an incredible weekend in Atlanta," Julie said. "Let me tell you about it." She flew to Atlanta with another friend and met two "old friends" of three or four years' duration. "We hardly left the hotel because we were having so much fun just spending time to-gether and getting reconnected. Except for meals and two dollars at TCBY, we hardly spent a cent!"

"Why?" I asked. "What made it such an incredible time? What did you *do?*"

She answered, "We spent the weekend talking, sharing and *getting to where the truth is between us.*"

I was hooked! I needed to hear the whole story. "Getting to where the truth is between us" is another way to talk about the principle of "unmasking" that we explored in chapter two.

Julie continued, "The fact is, these relationships turned a corner because we had Christ in the center and committed to one another in a way we never have before. Just a couple of years ago we spent a similar weekend in Atlanta, but all we did then was the tourist thing." What was different is that this second time they learned how to share their hearts with one another and were content with *being friends,* not merely *doing friendship.*

How many times have you been caught up in what I call "Day-Timer and travelogue" friendships? Friendships in which the conversation is a recap of your calendar and travels. "What have you been *doing* lately?" is the tell-tale question, or "Where have you *gone* lately?"

At an early season, informational conversations are a way of safely and slowly unmasking until deeper conversations can occur, but friendships can never go deep if our conversations stay shallow. Friend making takes time. It may happen that some rare friendships begin with startling rapidity, but they cannot be hurried. There are no shortcuts to time sharing in the development of deep friendships. Again, we may be startled by the quickness of our connection to another person, but we will discover, soon enough, that friend making requires times and seasons.

Seasons of Transition

Greg and Justin were very close friends in high school. They graduated together, spent time hanging out and learned to drink cappuccino together. They were closely knit and felt the deep value of the relationship—for a while. Then Greg got married, and their friendship began to get "inconvenient." Too much effort was involved, and Justin began to feel like a third wheel.

This is a critical season in a friendship, a bitter season in some. Some friends learn how to make the transition from singleness to the marriage of one or both. Many do not. Some choose to narrow the scope of their friendships and become much more exclusive in their relationship with husband or wife.

How do you make the transition from singleness to marriage? There is only one answer: you must work at it. You must communicate with each other, cut each other some slack and acknowledge that your relationship has changed—as it should. "Best friends" are naive to assume there will not come seasons of transition when their "best friend" marries another. As his spouse, he is naturally going to attach his affection, time and love on *her*. As her best friend, you cannot expect her to spend the same amount of time with you now that she's married. Changes are a natural part of life; *there are seasons to our friendships*.

"Let's get together . . ." has a hollow sound if the phone doesn't ring after the words are spoken. Some friends successfully make the transition by talking before the wedding about the changes that will likely take place and then meeting again some months later for a reality check. Perspective number four tells us the truth: change doesn't come easily, for it is hard, sometimes painful and often complicated; it need not, however, be fatal. *There are seasons to friendship*.

How can we make the transition from best single friends to single friend/married friend?

1. Talk about it. Do not simply assume you'll figure it out as you go. Work on it, together. Talk about it some more.

2. Don't talk about it. Spend some time together without "the paralysis of analysis." Get together and do what you did before

one of you got married. Enjoy the time you can spend together.

3. Think about your expectations and talk about them. Where friendships often get lost is when unstated expectations are not met and feelings get hurt.

4. Schedule some realistic times that will become sacred dates when you can meet.

5. Be realistic. Changes will occur and adjustments may take time.

6. The married person will probably need to take more of the initiative. Many single people are shy about interrupting their newly married friends.

Seasons of Change

Do you remember the movie *The Big Chill?* Okay, it was filled with the kitsch of the times and is better remembered for its music than its plot, but it shows a group of old college friends trying to decide in which season their friendships reside. Some try to pick up right where they left off, some have moved ahead of the group or beyond them, while others are sentimentally living back in the old days.

Bruce Springsteen's character in his song "Glory Days" is that kind of person. He lives back in the old days of high school or college and hasn't learned to move ahead to the seasons of life that will follow. Class reunions are a ritual way of sentimentalizing the past. They can be a wonderful time of doing reality checks on the seasons of friendships and helping people to let go, let up or move ahead. One thing was evident after the "Big Chill" weekend—people and relationships had changed!

This is reality: friends change, and so do friendships. Not every friendship will be a lifelong relationship that is cherished for its depth and longevity. Some friendships are merely functional contacts of people who happen to work together in the same place or live for a period of time together in the same neighborhood or residence hall on a campus. Some are short term and some may become lifelong, but expectations have a great deal to do with our feelings about them. There are people who hang on to every human contact as if their life and breath depend on this friendship, where every person is seen as a possible member of the permanent yearbook gallery of "best friends I have made."

We need to be honest when we talk about the season of change in friendship. Life's road divides before us and the journeys we take may lead to different places. There are intersections at which we watch wonderful friends veer to the west while we head eastward. Our prayer may always be that we will once again stand on common ground—sometimes there is the joy of such sweet reunions—but God may choose a different destination for our friends.

After six years of shared ministry, Steve and I parted as he stayed and I headed off to a new place and ministry. We parted not knowing if we would ever work together in ministry again. I knew the decision was a good step for me, maybe even a "right" step, but I was deeply homesick for the shared work we had known. A year later we did, in fact, stand again on the common ground of a shared ministry. In God's providence and design we joined up again, though we had let go before in a definite season of change.

What child hasn't stood watching as a friend climbed into the family car and moved to a new town or moved from the neighborhood across town to a new neighborhood, new apartment and new friends? In Western society today mobility is more common than stability. Change isn't easy and may cause pain, but there is joy to be found in every relationship. Helen Keller is quoted as having said, "With the death of every friend I love . . . a part of me has been buried . . . but their contribution to my being of happiness, strength and understanding remains to sustain me in an altered world."[2]

Seasons of Parting

When I was making the decision about leaving the state of Washington and a circle of dearly loved friends, I took a walk to a favorite place on the waterfront of Puget Sound. I sat one afternoon pondering my choices and the potential loss of friendships. I had met the night before with many of those friends to tell them of a job offer and get their advice. "What should I do? Which pathway will make the greatest use of my gifts? Can you see me having an effective ministry for the kingdom of God in this new role?" Thoughtfully and painfully, they affirmed the answer that was also forming in me: yes, I needed to go. Though it meant leaving them, they were honest people who listened for the voice of God and told me what they heard.

Now I stood on the shore and felt a lightheaded rush of excitement mixed with fear about these changes. I looked down at my feet and noticed the tide making its way in toward the shore. In it came and out it went. In and out. Ebb and flow. Just like my life. Just like friendships: they flourish and grow, they change and grow, and sometimes there is a separation. Kahil Gibran wrote, "When you part from your friend, you grieve not: For that which you love most in him may be clearer in his absence, as the mountain to the climber is clearer from the plain."[3]

When we learn to acknowledge the passing of life's seasons, we can learn to celebrate the transitions and see them as bridges to more of life, not less. Transitions typically involve three distinct stages: death, chaos, new life. There is an ending that is like a death for it creates loss and may be terminal to the relationship. There is often a time of chaos and pain, confusion and sadness; it is the murky time of transition. There will come a time of new life, new options and new friendships. It is yet another form of hospitality. To move ahead we must first move through seasons of transition and parting.

Seasons of Hospitality and Letting Go

Hebrews 13:2 counsels us, "Do not neglect to show hospitality to strangers, for by doing that some have entertained angels without knowing it." The Rule of Saint Benedict, chapter 53, says, "Let all guests who arrive be received like Christ, for He is going to say, 'I came as a guest and you received me.'" Once again the concept of "hospitality" proves a lively image for the inevitable changes that come to all friendships.

The German word for hospitality is *Gastfreundschaft,* which literally translated is "friendship for the guest." Think about what you do before a guest arrives to spend time with you. What steps do you take to prepare for an important visitor? A good host provides helpful clues for understanding the season of hospitality and assessing the time for letting go. "Friendship for the guest" typically includes four specific activities.

Housecleaning. At my house, typically, the first thing we do is some housecleaning; we create a sense of order in the home. Margaret Guenther says,

> We must know ourselves well, both our dark corners and our airless spaces—the spots where dust collects and mold begins to grow. It is not enough to push our rubbish into the closet and shut the door, nor to lower blinds and dim the lights so the dirt doesn't show, although these are tempting tricks for harried caretakers of houses and of souls. No, we must clear our house, and then keep cleaning it so that we have a worthy place when we invite others to rest and refreshment.[4]

Invitation and welcome. "We invite someone into a space that offers safety and shelter and put our own needs aside, as everything is focused on the comfort and refreshment of the guest."[5] That is the welcome of hospitality, the friendship of the guest. In practical terms that means the following:

☐ Time and space should be inviting, welcoming, safe and secure from interruptions.

☐ Time is given. We choose to make room in schedules, energy, listening and love. We choose to create open space that is as uncluttered as possible and thus as available to the guest as we can make it.

☐ Confidentiality is assured. A friend must feel safe from judgment, exposure, criticism or rejection, whatever the topic may be. We must never forget that people's secrets are precious and should be treated with much respect.

Listening and storytelling. Hospitality includes a time of storytelling and requires attentive listening—without initial interjections of our very enlightening and interesting experiences that coincide with theirs. Good hosts can set aside their own need to dominate the conversation and will listen instead to the stories, needs and directions of the guests.

Of course, all good storytelling is ultimately a dialogue, but telling our own stories should be done sparingly and with great care. We simply must resist the temptation to play the game of one-upmanship in our stories. Sometimes we need to say gently, "This time is yours; let's talk about you for a while first." Our task as a host is attentive listening by inviting the telling of stories around the campfire, dinner table, coffee cup or pizza. Only after careful, attentive and reflective listening do we begin to point out new sights along the way and even to share stories of our own journeys down a similar road.

Limits are recognized. Finally, all good hospitality recognizes that the guest will be "ours" for only a short time. We must then let them go to the next stop on their journey. The friendship need not end, but active involvement in day-to-day life may lessen or cease.

A good host recognizes that she may not necessarily keep the person in her home forever—the person may need to move on ahead to the next station, place or phase of her life. Hospitality means that we make room for changes of all kinds in the relationship. A wise host allows the other person to move ahead when it is time to let up, without letting go.

As one of my friends said to me, "You know, I have finally figured it out after several painful and traumatic experiences with people: friendships change and that's okay. I don't need to hang on to every friend as if the change means we have failed. Friendships change and that's okay." As life moves us onward, so our friendships will experience changes. A good host knows when it's time to say good-bye and assist someone to move on to their next destination.

Seasons of Closure

How do you know when it's time to bring closure to a friendship and move ahead? I believe the necessary step is for one of you to unmask and ask honest questions about the relationship. You are likely to discern whether the friendship matters enough to invest in it or not. Assessing the value of the friendship requires asking some hard questions. Elsewhere I called this "the Dean Witter principle" because I believe there comes a time of practical and careful investment *or* it may be time to sell the stock. Some of the same questions are pertinent.

☐ Is it worth the continuing expenditure of my resources (of time and energy)?

☐ Is it worth the risks involved?

☐ Do we see a mutual future in it?

☐ Am I merely hanging on for old time's sake and not wisely discerning that it's time to sell and reinvest my resources elsewhere?

What are some good reasons to bring closure to a relationship or at least acknowledge that change is imperative? First, the natural setting in which the relationship began has changed and will not likely change back (for example, you graduate, get a new job or get married). Second, there are diminishing returns in the relationship—what once brought you joy and satisfaction has now become an empty ritual.

What are some bad reasons to bring closure? Some people wrongly think that conflict in and of itself is always wrong; avoiding upset is not reason enough to conclusively end a friendship. In addition, personal emotional trauma or transition are vulnerable moments to make major relational decisions. Finally, new interest in a developing friendship may be another vulnerable time to bring closure to old friendships. The novelty of the new may merely signal that it's time to reinvest more activity in the old.

Nevertheless, closure must come to many relationships in the natural flow of life. Ken Gire describes this familiarity of saying goodby:

> In moving to a new house, we have to say good-bye to the old neighborhood, old friends, old memories. In going off to college, we have to leave our home and family behind. In getting married, we have to shed something of our independence. In starting a career, we have to leave behind college and those special times, those special friends, that cloistered sense of security. In starting a family, we have to close the chapter on the relatively uncomplicated, uninterrupted life we had as a childless couple. In getting a promotion, we have to leave behind a job we love, maybe or a city we love, or a state. In our children going off to college or to careers or to start families of their own, something is left behind when they leave, something precious, something we and they can come back to only in stories and scrapbooks. In retiring we bid a final farewell to our livelihood, and though our friends at work remain our friends, a dimension of those friendships is also left behind.
>
> We go from threshold to threshold with something pulling us forward and something pulling us back.[6]

Study Questions

1. How do you respond to the concept of "seasons of friendship"?

2. Can you identify seasons in one of your current friendships?

3. What other advice would you add to the list for transitions in single best friends to single friend/married friend?

4. What have you learned about letting go of friends in your life? Did those lessons come from painful experiences?

5. What recent transitions have you made in one of your important friendships?

Six

Iron Sharpens Iron

I've dreamed of meeting her all of my life . . . a
bosom friend—an intimate friend, you know—a
really kindred spirit to whom I can confide my
inmost soul.
LUCY MAUD MONTGOMERY

Mutual encouragement is the glue for healthy relationships.

*I*N A FILE FOLDER IN MY DESK DRAWER IS A FOLDER THAT I
open only rarely, but when it is necessary the office door closes
and I open that secret file. When that file comes out, the need is
great and the results are certain. Stuffed and overstuffed is a
folder full of notes, cards, letters and memos sent from people
across the years. Some notes are good for the moment, but some
are "keepers." When I am down or feeling uncertain and need
some strength, I go to my keeper folder for courage. It inevitably
makes me smile and lifts my heart.

My friend Steve Moore is one of the best encouragers I know.
He doesn't just say "atta boy" or "keep up the good work," he
sends notes like the following. Think about how *you* would feel

getting a note like this!

Keith, that was an amazing presentation today; you were meek and winsome and you left no escape whatsoever. The biblical writer James would have been pleased. Thanks for giving us the truth, especially when I have a pretty good idea what it will cost you as a teacher to have said it.

The writer of Proverbs said, "Iron sharpens iron, and one person sharpens the wits of another" (Prov 27:17). This is the principle of mutual encouragement, biblical perspective number five: *mutual encouragement is the glue for healthy relationships.*

One of the most significant acts of love I can give another person is a word of encouragement. When I encourage you I say, "You matter to me, I value you, I honor you, you are significant to me." Encouragement can be oral (spoken words of affirmation), written (a note or card), physical (a hug or smile) or symbolic (a gift). In other words, encouragement may be spoken or shown, but its message communicates deeply to the spirit or soul of another in such a way that he or she is transformed.

Barnabas was given a name that many could share; it literally means "son of encouragement." Barnabas was that for Paul. He dared to stand alongside Paul before anyone knew God had chosen the unlikely candidate for the task of worldwide missions. He brought Paul into the fellowship when he was still considered an enemy and told the community to welcome him as a brother into the fellowship. He stood up again for young John Mark later when he had experienced a publicly humiliating failure and needed to be restored to the community. He had a contagious spirit of generosity about him. He was an advocate for the grace of encouragement.

For years I thought of Barnabas as the great encourager, the one who stood alone to bring encouragement to others out of the goodness of his own heart. What I have seen more clearly in recent years is that Barnabas's name probably contains a clue to the source of his great capacity for encouragement, for he was the *son of encouragement*, one whose own life had been richly filled with encouragement from another, perhaps his own father. The early church recognized a quality or passion for encouragement in Barnabas and gave him that nickname. Barnabas brought something to Paul and many others, something he drew out of the deep wells of his own life. Can you identify one person in your life who has been that voice of encouragement for you?

Encouraging another person literally replenishes the courage that has been dissipated, used, spent or lost. It refills low or empty tanks with the fresh fuel of courage. That is the meaning of the word, encouragement. Its converse sharpens the meaning even further: to *dis*courage is to drain the tanks of courage in another person, to create a slow or fast leak in the supply of a precious commodity.

Two of my best student leaders just gave me a wonderful gift after their commencement. Kim and Heather provided outstanding leadership in the area of public worship on our campus. For a year they guided major programs that affected the entire college community. Their gift to me was a picture of them taken at commencement. The best part of the gift are the five words engraved across the bottom of the frame: "Thanks for believing in us."

What created that response in them? When these two women started as leaders, they were good musicians, had a strong track record in leadership and were passionate about the job, but it didn't occur to me until I received their gift that they had felt uncertain or doubtful about their abilities. Encouragement fills that need for confidence and trust in us. I believed in them and told them so. Encouragement is empowerment; it energizes people in a way that nothing else can do. Friends offer empowering encouragement to one another.

Encouragement is a voice saying "yes" when life is saying

"NO!" It is an energizing, revitalizing power most often spoken in simple words like "Go for it," "You can do it," "I believe in you" and "We're behind you all the way." What encouragement gives is like increased octane, a richer mix of fuel; it enhances the power because it infuses my confidence with yours, creating the "something more" of courage to risk, venture and dare.

It was Kerry Strug at the 1996 Summer Olympics, courageously taking that final jump with a badly sprained ankle, who gave the U.S. Women's Gymnastic Team the gold medal. Her grit combined with the confidence of teammates, coaches and parents gave her the something more of a champion gymnast.

Isn't encouragement merely a kind of mutual deception where two people just tell each other what they think the other wants to hear? Encouragement is not flattery. In flattery I deceive you with false information rather than empower you with the truth. Encouragement is when I speak truth to you because I love you. Flattery is giving insincere or empty compliments. Friendship requires the nutrients of honesty and truth in which encouragement is rooted.

Truth Telling Is Friend Making

I believe that God intends the church to be a community of mentors, a community of friends familiar with speaking words of confirmation and contradiction. I prefer the experience of confirmation more than the words of contradiction, but I understand that both are needed in the work of mentorship and friendship and have come to understand that both are aspects of encouragement. What I find so energizing is that the Bible offers numerous pictures of both.

In the book of Esther we meet Mordecai, uncle to the young Jewish queen, Esther. Mordecai is a great paradigm for the community of faith as an example of the mentor-friend. His gift to Esther and Israel was that he found ways to affirm, confirm and support his kinswoman. He took her aside and validated her with his words: "Perhaps you have come to royal dignity for just such a time as this." He treated her as the competent young adult she was. He didn't tell her what her task was. He didn't delineate every step she needed to take to save her people. He respectfully acknowledged her own ability to think.

But he did not try merely to make her feel good about herself; rather he issued a challenge to her that required a contradiction of the status quo. He challenged her to use her new-found power to help her people. "Perhaps you have come to power for just such a time as this." Esther's time was a time of great danger for her people. The Jews were generally not people of privilege among the Medes and Persians. They had been shut up, shut down and shut out of places of power—until Esther. And Mordecai came to her with a word of challenge, a word that would test her faith. He warned her, "Do not think that in the king's palace you will escape any more than all the other Jews. For if you keep silence at such a time as this, relief and deliverance will rise for the Jews from another quarter, but you and your father's family will perish. Who knows? Perhaps you have come to royal dignity for just such a time as this" (Esther 4:13-14).

A friend is one who provides confirmation when needed and challenge or contradiction when *that* is needed. Friendship is not the flattery of telling us only what we *want* to hear; it is also telling us what we *need* to hear. Mordecai's words challenged young Esther to take a stand expressed in what is perhaps the bravest statement in all of Holy Scripture: "I will go to the king, though it is against the law; and if I perish, I perish" (4:16). Her task was clearly set before her.

How did that task become so clear to young Queen Esther? First, when Mordecai offered his word as her mentor. Second, when Esther invited others to join her in fasting and prayer. "I and my maids will also fast as you do" (4:16). Encouragement belongs to the community of friends. We cannot run this race all alone. We cannot do the work God has given us to do all by ourselves. I once heard a sermon that quoted Suzan Johnson: "We need others to walk and run with us." Those others are friends who see that we need to hear truth and are willing to *en-courage* us with words of truth.

Friends tell us the truth about who we are, encouraging us and helping us grow. Someone has said there are only two people who will tell you the truth, your enemy who hates you and your friend who loves you. Your enemy tells you the truth to hurt you, but your friend tells you the truth for your growth. To encourage can mean either affirmation or confrontation, acceptance or contradiction, the grace of hope or the grace of honest critique—but always encouragement is grounded in truth telling. Who in your life is your greatest friend-critic, the one who will tell you the truth in order that you will grow? To whom are you a friend-critic?

Todd was my mentor in friendship though he is twenty years my junior. He was a student who somehow connected to my teaching style and took every course I taught. I have often accused him of having a substandard education because he was warped by too many "Anderson credit hours" on his transcript, but we developed a strong and meaningful friendship.

After a time of unmasking through class discussions and informal meetings, he decided he needed me as his mentor, and we formalized the relationship. As we met in my office, I became a sounding board for many ideas as the voice of the wise older friend whose insights could provide correctives to the follies of youth. I suppose there was some truth in the last sentence you just read, but more accurately we found ourselves standing on the holy ground of mutual encouragement. Week after week we met to share our lives with one another and to reach across the differences of age, experience and education to discover common ground, which was transformed into sacred space by our mutual encouragement.

But I was and am a busy man. Sometimes I would miss our appointments because of my very full and important schedule. Sometimes I would announce to Todd that I had to cut it short because of a crucial meeting or an unexpected appointment.

One morning Todd invited me to meet for our appointment at his dorm room. He shut the door and said, "I will not let you get away with it anymore. You have agreed that what we do is important, but you continually blow it off and treat it as something less than it is. I will not let you get away with discounting our time anymore!"

I don't think I ever did again. Todd taught me through the power of contradiction. To say yes to some things means we will say no to other things. If we do not learn that in our friendships, they will surely fail. If we only say yes there will be nothing left to give anyone. If we only say no we will have plenty of time and energy but no friends. Todd taught me that because he valued words more than I did and took my words to mean what I said they meant. Do you have at least one person in your life who will tell you the truth, even if it hurts?

Real friends don't lie to each other—the friendship matters too much for even polite dishonesty. Real friends understand that truth is like sunshine and water to tender young plants: it feeds and gives growth. The notion that friends care for one another by "protecting" them from truth is a dangerous deception.

Darin worked as an accountant for a national firm that was in serious financial crisis. He had access to information regarding the extent of the company's situation but was told by his boss to keep the information hidden and quiet and even to withhold certain facts from their creditors. At their weekly accountability and prayer time, Darin told his friend Craig his struggle. "I don't know what to do when they tell me to lie," he said.

"Of course you do," replied Craig. "It just won't be easy, but as a Christian your options do not include lying or unethical business practices. If you can't do your job without crossing those lines, you need a new job!"

Darin felt the truth of those words as they fit his own struggling conscience, and his path became clear. Even in his trauma he was grateful for a friend like Craig whose encouragement came in the form of truth telling.

Dale, on the other hand, resented his friend James when he confronted him with truth in a similar situation. He was outraged, claiming that James had turned his back on him in the middle of the crisis rather than standing by him when he needed him most. Two months later Dale was fired for his actions when a new owner took over the company. In his anger and deceit he lost a job and a good friend. He mistook contradiction for rejection rather than a truth-telling expression of encouragement.

You Honor Me When You Speak Truth

Romans 12:10 says, "Love one another with mutual affection; outdo one another in showing honor." Encouragement and truth telling are the means by which we honor another above ourselves. There is power in encouragement unlike anything else. It literally transforms us from weakness into strength, from fear into faith, from defeat into victory. C. S. Lewis says,

> Alone among unsympathetic companions, I hold certain views and standards timidly, half ashamed to avow them and half doubtful if they can after all be right. Put me back among my Friends and in half an hour—in ten minutes—these same views and standards become once more indisputable. The opinion of this little circle, while I am in it, outweighs those of a thousand outsiders: as Friendship strengthens, it will do this even when my Friends are far away. . . . Men who have real Friends are less easy to manage or "get at"; harder for good Authorities to correct or for bad Authorities to corrupt.[1]

Lewis reminds us of the dangers of friendship, which can be a school either of virtue or of vice but whose power is indisputable. Everyone has an inner circle of friends whose opinion matters the most and whose words of encouragement bring the greatest courage. That encouragement can lead us to the very best or the very worst.

When I was about eleven, a new kid moved into the neighborhood. He seemed pretty cool to me and my best friend, Phil, so we let him join us in our well-established friendship—at least we were ready to give him a try. We let him hang out with us as we rode our bikes and played baseball in the wide open spaces of South Park, near my home.

John was doing okay for a new kid and seemed to be passing the test in the rites of passage into friendship as required by eleven-year-old boys. But Phil and I had an unspoken understanding that leadership was shared in our friendship. We took turns. It led to a fight only once, which I lost, though I got a couple of good shots in on him as he wore his new white Levis and light-colored shirt. The grass stains would never come out—I saw to that! John, on the other hand, didn't know "the rules." How could he? We never talked about them. If he did know them he disagreed with them and made his own. To tell the truth, his "suggestions" for us became more and more frequent and began to feel like demands.

It came to a major crossroads one day when John announced we were taking a ride to the grocery store. "Let's get some candy bars," he said. I failed to notice at the time that he didn't use a word for purchase. "Watch me carefully," he said. "I'll show you how it's done."

As we stood in line we learned what he meant by "get." What I saw both mesmerized and scandalized me and—in that instant, in some truly profound way—my life was transformed as I watched him slip a Chunky candy bar into his jacket pocket. My heart raced wildly and pounded so loudly that I was sure everyone in the store could hear it.

Outside he said, "You can do it too!" I didn't try it that day, and I don't think Phil did either, but we were awed by John's brazen act of shoplifting and joined him soon enough in our own successful careers of minor crime. My friendship with John caused me to compromise some basic values and beliefs. The memory lasted for years; the friendship did not. It was too much of a compromise; we felt too trapped by John's dominance and soon lost interest in him altogether.

John's choices empowered my choices and taught me early enough that sometimes friends lead friends astray. For some there is encouragement and a nudge to the good, but for others there is empowerment for compromise and betrayal. Friendships can encourage us to take the low road as well as the high road.

I was fascinated by a story of a group of Christians out for an evening of a movie and pizza. Only moments into the film they all realized it was a violent, sadistic and sexually exploitive movie that offended their individual Christian sensibilities. They all agreed later that it was unworthy of their time, but, to a person, they kept silent in the theater, not willing to be the one to "blow the whistle" and offend the rest of the group. Rather than act as voices of conscience and encouragement for the best, they chose the road of silent compromise.

For decades much of the church has kept silent on issues of race and poverty, in some places only grudgingly ready to declare racial reconciliation as an essential part of kingdom living. We call "prophetic" those who stand against the stream of spiritual blindness and cultural conformity to speak words of biblical truth. Encouragement is the sometimes costly word of contradiction spoken to people we value *about things that matter.* Encouragement can be a word of challenge to help us see our blind spots, individually or as a congregation. Contradiction and confirmation are not opposites! They are the two sides of a coin that is a precious gift given by host and guest alike. Consider these scriptural exhortations:

☐ "Better is open rebuke than hidden love" (Prov 27:5).

☐ "Well meant are the wounds a friend inflicts" (Prov 27:6).

☐ "Do not let the sun go down on your anger" (Eph 4:26).

☐ "Love covers a multitude of sins" (1 Peter 4:8).

☐ "Confess your sins to one another" (James 5:16).

When Do We Most Need Truth Telling?

When we have betrayed our truest values and compromised our convictions. At such times we are vulnerable to the insidious sin of pride and the danger of denial.

When we have succeeded and "are on a roll." At such times we are even more vulnerable to a pride that will cause us to forget that we rarely succeed without the supportive cast of others.

When we have been hurt by another and are caught in the cycle of anger-blame-defensiveness-and-revenge. Blame seldom sits only on one side of the street, but even if it belongs fully across the road, we must think about the future with the one who has hurt us. I heard of an office manager who ran into a conflict with his office staff and things got tense. He was blamed for some things that hurt him and gave him ammunition for entering the cycle of defensiveness and revenge but he tried a different approach. The next day he brought a construction worker's hard hat to the office and posted a sign on his door: Construction zone, enter at your own risk. His actions defused a potentially risky and hostile situation.

When we are too busy, too distracted, too scattered to listen carefully. If we have stopped listening well, we are susceptible to the loss of the perspective that a friend can give us. If the only voice we hear is our own, then we are in danger of great failure.

When we have hurt our friend, intentionally or unintentionally. We can see it in their eyes or feel it in their reaction—we caused them pain. Maybe we didn't know our words would create such a response or maybe we wanted to get in one little "dig" to make up for some earlier hurt we felt. But we hurt our friend.

When we are uncertain about the health of our friendship. I recall the day I pulled a friend aside and said, "Here's how it looks to me, my friend. I don't know if I've missed something important or if you haven't been very open with me, but I feel like we're creating a barrier of some kind between us and I don't want that to happen. Help me understand what's going on." When I spoke those words to a very close friend, I didn't know the outcome of my words but felt deeply what I said. After twelve years of friendship, you'd expect it would be easier than it was, but we're both fairly private people. Conversations like this aren't natural for our personalities. What mattered is that we looked each other in the eye, had the conversation, cleared the air and removed the debris in our relationship.

Encouragement comes in many forms, two of which are words of assurance and of truth telling, words of confirmation and of contradiction. Christina Rosetti wrote about this idea in *Goblin Market* in 1862:

> For there is no friend like a sister
> In calm or stormy weather;
> To cheer one on the tedious way,
> To fetch one if one goes astray,
> To lift one if one totters down,
> To strengthen whilst one stands.

Affirmation, encouragement and validation are sometimes more necessary than criticism. I sat down at dinner with a national leader in the movement for justice. I was uncertain about some decisions I had made because of criticism that had come my way from another person in leadership. I poured out my heart and my intentions, and my friend said to me, "My son, don't you let anybody cause you to feel deflated or discouraged. Don't you let anybody invalidate what you're trying to do for the kingdom of

God." His words were like a breath of pure oxygen to a man choking for air. He encouraged me with his love and support. Sometimes we need to be confirmed.

At other times we will need a friend to help us remove our blinders in order to see the whole horizon. A former student of mine came to see me and was ecstatic. For years he had suffered from an ailment that blurred his vision and caused chronic headaches because both his eyes couldn't focus on the same object. Surgery and new glasses had finally brought healing to him. He shouted, "The greatest thing in the world is to be able to see clearly!" Truth telling gives clear vision to what has become cloudy or blinded in relationships. It is pure grace.

In the Midnight Hour

Martin Luther King Jr. told the story of the bleakest hour of his campaign for civil rights. He was in the thick of the conflicted Montgomery bus boycott when he received a phone call that threatened his life unless he gave it up and left town. That night he heard the voice of God within telling him, "Martin Luther, stand up for righteousness. Stand up for justice. Stand up for truth. And lo I will be with you even until the end of the earth."[2]

That voice *empowered* him, but it was the voice of Mother Pollard, an elderly woman who was an active part of the movement, that *encouraged* him three days later.

"Something is wrong with you," said Pollard. "You didn't talk strong tonight."

"Oh, no, Mother Pollard," King replied, "Nothing is wrong. I am feeling as fine as ever."

"Now you can't fool me," she said. "I knows something is wrong. Is it that we ain't doing things to please you? Or is that the white folks is bothering you." . . . Before he could say anything, she moved her face close to his and said loudly, "I done *told* you we is with you all the way. But even if we ain't with you, God's gonna take care of you." . . . Later, King said that with her consoling words fearlessness had come over him in the form of raw energy.[3]

In the tone and timbre of a human voice, we can sometimes hear most clearly the voice of God. Encouragement is the glue that will hold together friendships that run deep.

Study Questions

1. What was the greatest word of encouragement you ever received from anyone? What was the setting? How did it encourage you?

2. Who is the greatest encourager you have ever known?

3. When was the last time you spoke a word of encouragement to someone? What were the results?

4. What are you discouraged about in your life right now? What would make a positive difference in your situation?

5. Who tells you the truth in your life?

Seven

Friends Fail Friends

Grace is the ultimate act of empathy. It is possible
on the human level only to the degree that we can
imagine ourselves in other people's shoes.
DANIEL TAYLOR

Forgiveness is the indispensable skill for any healthy relationship.

*I*F YOU LOVE A PERSON LONG ENOUGH, HE OR SHE WILL
disappoint you, hurt you or even leave you. I wish it could be
different but our humanness doesn't seem to let us get away with
perfection. I read recently that the only place perfection exists is
on our résumés! Simple day-to-day life creates stress, disappointment, frustration, hurt, conflict and anger between even the best
of friends.

Think about your current circle of friends. Is there even one
who has never disappointed or hurt you? Has there ever been a
friendship in your life that lasted longer than six months without
some pain or wall or conflict, however large or small? I know that
the famous friendships of the movie world lead us to believe
otherwise but even the Lone Ranger and Tonto must have had
some conflicts, Batman and Robin some disagreements, Ozzie
and Harriet some moments of pain. Biblical perspective number

six tells us: *forgiveness is the indispensable skill for any healthy relation-ship*. It is essential because friends fail friends.

The Teacher Gets an *F!*

We return to our old friends Paul and Barnabas, but this time we will highlight their relationship with a mutual friend, John Mark. Barnabas and Paul had a strong working relationship and apparently a good friendship. In the early days of the church, Barnabas, the encourager, introduced Paul to the community and was a broker of credibility and welcome. They shared missionary travels together and were effectively used by God through their partnership. The real crisis developed over their young protégé John Mark. John Mark was known well by both and apparently seen by both as a young man with a future, a young man with potential for the work of the kingdom of God, until he failed Paul on a missionary journey and asked to be sent home. We're not told if he got in over his head or if the struggles were too intense for his young faith, but he bailed out on Paul and left him without support at a crucial time in the ministry. We learn much about the flawed and weak humanity of this young man at this threshold moment in the early days of his ministry.

In the aftermath of this episode, we also learn a great deal about the humanity of Paul, the older, mature, veteran leader. Paul refused to take Mark on another excursion; in fact he was downright stubborn about it all. Paul, the great teacher of the church, was unwilling to accept Mark's failure, help him learn from it and see it as an opportunity for growth! In Acts 15:37-39 we read, "Barnabas wanted to take with them John called Mark. But Paul decided not to take with them one who had deserted them in Pamphylia and had not accompanied them in the work. The disagreement became so sharp that they parted company."

Friends fail friends. John Mark failed Paul but, in the sharp disagreement with Barnabas, Paul failed twice—once with his long-time friend Barnabas and again with his young student, John Mark. This time the teacher deserved the *F*. Barnabas, ever the encourager, took the side of young John Mark. He wanted Paul to give the young man a break, though he had disappointed them; he wanted Paul to do for John Mark what Barnabas had done for Paul years earlier, to forgive him. This time, however, Paul, the great theologian of reconciliation and forgiveness, refused. It led to a major rift in their friendship, one that could be healed only by forgiveness.

This triangle of relational difficulties illustrates one important point: friendships don't always work out neatly because there are times of struggle and conflict. Friends fail friends. Conflicts follow failures and create reservoirs of mistrust and hurt. Barnabas and Paul were in conflict, Paul and John Mark were in conflict, and everyone around them was affected by their struggles. The residual effects of relational conflicts can be deadly to those who happen to get in the way of the fallout. Paul's relationship with John Mark was torn by Mark's failure and a subsequent refusal by Paul to forgive him. We don't know if the torn relationships were ever restored.

How could that happen? Paul and Barnabas were one of the greatest ministry teams in biblical history. Who better than those two to model forgiveness, restoration and reconciliation? Who better than those two to show us a friendship that would finish the course? Anyone would nominate the early Paul and Barnabas for the "friends of the year" award. At one time they were models of a great partnership but then anger and conflict intruded in an invasive, almost violent way. Every friendship is vulnerable to the tear caused by disagreement, dissent, discord or conflict. Even the best of friendships is vulnerable.

No Middle Ground

Friends for life are those rare people who have learned one of two skills that may surprise you: the skill of dishonesty or of forgiveness. I don't believe there is a middle ground. Either you learn to be dishonest about hurt, pain and disappointment that happens between two people or you learn to forgive one another because human beings cause each other pain. There are degrees of disagreement and disappointment that range from mild to extreme just as there are degrees to our experience of physical pain, but conflict is the soil in which relationships grow, the ecosystem in which people live and die. Happy endings are possible but dependent, I believe, on learning the skill of forgiveness. There are people all around us, friends in fact, whose sharp edges cut or bruise us. There are friends all around us whose inattention or preoccupations cause us frustration or even suffering. There are friends whose neglect burdens us with gloomy depression or tired hearts. Forgiveness is an indispensable skill in any healthy relationship but doesn't come naturally to most of us. You will need to forgive your friends and your friends will need to forgive you—it's a basic and frequent fact of life.

Forgiveness is difficult because it requires a tenderized spirit, which is more difficult to maintain in the midst of conflict than at other times. The moments when we need to be most tender are those very moments when our anger or hurt takes over and causes a callous to grow over our spirits, a hardening of the heart when a softening is the only way to reconciliation. Forgiveness is tough enough in the best of situations and with the best of friends; it is tougher yet when stress, weariness and trauma complicate the situation and muddy the clear mind of friendship.

What is forgiveness? Think first about what it is *not*.

☐ *Forgetting*. It is not forgiveness if I stifle it, deliberately attempting to forget the wrong. Memories are like data permanently stored on our mental disk drives. We cannot and probably should not suppress or "delete" memories too easily. Memory helps us to grow deeper as we make peace with them. Frederick Buechner has some wise thoughts on memory.

> The sad things that happened long ago will always remain part of who we are just as the glad and gracious things will too, but instead of being a burden of guilt, recrimination, and regret that make us constantly stumble as we go, even the saddest things can become, once we have made peace with them, a source of wisdom and strength for the journey that still lies ahead. It is through memory that we are able to reclaim much of our lives that we have long since written off by finding that in everything that has happened to us over the years God was offering us possibilities of new life and healing which, though we may have missed them at the time, we can still choose and be brought to life by and healed by all these years later.[1]

Forgiveness doesn't ever say, "Forget it, it didn't matter anyway." When friends fail friends, it is serious, it does matter and only forgiveness is powerful enough to heal the memory and transform it into growth.

☐ *Pretending.* It is not forgiveness when I pretend that nothing's wrong, as if you can't possibly hurt me. Forgiveness is the act of honestly facing the wrong, hurt or pain and dealing with it. Pretense is a way of protecting against vulnerability. Forgiveness is a way of restoring relationships by facing up to the failure, beginning with open eyes and honest words: "I am sorry, I was wrong. I failed you and I confess it to you now."

☐ *Ignoring.* It is not forgiveness if I simply overlook the issue and "just get on with it," as if nothing has happened. Some people are skilled at this strategy of deceit and treat it as politeness or good Christian humility when it is, in fact, dishonesty. A conspiracy of silence between friends doesn't bring reconciliation to a relationship; it brings a cloud cover of more dishonesty.

☐ *Discounting.* It is not forgiveness if I reduce the cost to me or you as if the pain or loss were less than they were. It is best characterized by the overused and trivialized comment invoked almost daily among some groups of people, "Whatever." It epito-mizes the lack of commitment and conviction that some suggest is the norm for the twentysomethings today. It is the mark of a discounted conversation because it doesn't take the other person or the experience seriously. Forgiveness cost Jesus the cross, he did not look at our rebellious sin and say, "Whatever!"

When Jesus acted to forgive errant behavior he took the behavior seriously, without condoning or making light of it. He loved people enough to remove the evil or sinful action so that it no longer remained a barrier to the relationship. When we forgive as Jesus did, we will not let the hurtful act remain as a mental block to our friendship. It means that we are reconciled, brought together once again. Forgiveness is usually costly to the one giving it for the forgiver agrees to carry the hurt away from the one who caused it. The forgiver agrees that the pain will not be allowed to remain an open and constant wound. Forgiveness is deeply spiritual because the deepest hurt in a relationship is most often the blow to one's spirit. The forgiver will not let that hurt create a permanent fracture but acts instead to set the broken bone and allow the slow work of healing.

I remember vividly one person's response to forgiveness. She said, "I don't feel worthy to be forgiven." But that's the point, exactly. Forgiveness is an act of grace offered to one who has wronged you. Buechner said, "For both parties, forgiveness means the freedom again to be at peace inside their own skins and to be glad in each other's presence."[2]

I have no illusion that forgiveness is easy or natural. It is neither, but it is the necessary skill to be learned by all who would become good friends to others.

For-give-ness

Walter Wangerin writes persuasively about forgiveness as irra-tional and unwise because, he says, "For-give-ness is a holy, complete, unqualified *giving*. . . . Forgiveness is a willing relinquishment of certain rights. The one sinned against chooses *not* to demand her rights of redress for the hurt she has suffered."[3] He then tells a wonderful story of his experience of the hurt that necessitates forgiveness through a painful tear in his relationship with his wife, Thanne.

> Thanne could not forgive me. This is a plain fact. My sin was greater than her capacity to forgive, had lasted longer than her kindness, had grown more oppressive than her goodness. This was not a single act nor a series of acts, but my being. My sin was the murder of her spirit, the unholy violation of her sole identity—the blithe assumption of her presence, as though she were furniture. I had broken her. How could a broken person be at the same time whole enough to forgive? No: Thanne was created finite and could not forgive me.
>
> But Jesus could.
>
> One day Thanne stood in the doorway of my study, looking at me. I turned in my chair and saw that she was not angry. Small Thanne, delicate, diminutive Thanne, she was not glaring but gazing at me with gentle, questioning eyes. This was totally unexpected, both her presence and her expression. There was no reason why she should be standing there, no detail I've forgotten to tell you. Yet for a full minute we looked at one another; and then she walked to my side where I sat. She touched my shoulder. She said, "Wally, will you hug me?"
>
> I leaped from my chair. I wrapped her all around in my two arms and squeezed my wife, my wife, so deeply in my body—and we both burst into tears.
>
> Would I hug her? Oh, but the better question was, would she *let* me hug her? And she did.
>
> Dear Lord Jesus, where did this come from, this sudden, unnatural, undeserved willingness to let me touch her, hug her, love her? Not from me! I was her ruination. Not from her,

because I had killed that part of her. From you!

How often had we hugged before? I couldn't count the times. How good has those hugs been? I couldn't measure the goodness. But *this* hug—don't you know, it was my salvation, different from any other and more remarkable because this is the hug I should never had. *That* is forgiveness! The law was gone. Rights were all abandoned. Mercy took their place. We were married again. And it was you, Christ Jesus, in my arms—within my graceful Thanne. One single, common hug, and we were alive again.

Thanne gave me a gift: She gave me the small plastic figure of a woman with her eyes rolled up, her mouth skewed to one side, the tongue lolling out, a cartoon face. I have this gift in my study today.

The inscription at the bottom reads: *I love you so much it hurts.*[4] Forgiveness gives life to that which is too often left for dead, reconciles relationships that are beyond hope, rebuilds that which has been leveled by the tornadolike winds of conflict and offers the single greatest gift offered another human being: one more chance. The love of marriage hurts as does the love of friendship; that is why learning to forgive is the quintessential skill in relationships.

Forgiveness is the skill of communicating grace when relationships are at their most fragile and vulnerable. It depends on another skill, that of truth telling. There are movements today attempting to call people across the land back to a commitment to basic values, core beliefs and clearly articulated convictions. Essential to these movements is a commitment to accountability groups in which one friend holds another friend accountable for faithfully living up to those values. Instead of the competition and fear that can become hostility, there is the integrity that grows out of mutual encouragement and mutual truth telling. Truth telling has become such an unusual virtue in our world today that it needs cheerleaders and supporters to keep it in the game!

In 1784 William Blake wrote these words in his poem "A Poison Tree":

I was angry with my friend;
I told my wrath, my wrath did end.
I was angry with my foe;
I told it not, my wrath did grow.

Truth telling is when I value you enough to speak the truth as I see it to you in order to help you grow.

Forgiveness requires honesty or it is another form of mask-wearing. Forgiveness assumes truth telling, critique or confrontation, but how do I know when I am "doing it right"? Alice Miller writes, "If it is very painful for you to criticize your friends, then you are safe in doing it. But if you take the slightest pleasure in it, that is the time to hold your tongue."[5]

In Ephesians Paul gives the advice "Be angry but do not sin." Clearly the sin is not in the anger itself. Some anger is legitimate, appropriate or necessary. Truth telling, even in anger, is not in itself sinful but it can lead to the healing of forgiveness. There is no sin in anger. Anger can be righteous and justified, deserved and necessary. There is, however, I believe, sin in anger that does not seek reconciliation. That is why forgiveness is such an indispensable skill for our relationships. Forgiveness is the container that carries reconciliation between two people.

The Costs of Forgiveness

I won't say to you that forgiveness follows a four-point outline. But here are four common—though costly—markers of giving forgiveness.

1. Forgiveness costs an acknowledgment of the wrong, otherwise known as truth telling. I need to acknowledge to myself and to you that I have done wrong.

2. Forgiveness costs a sense of sorrow and penitence over the

wrong that has been done. I must not only acknowledge that something wrong happened; I must not only be sorry that I got caught or that it hurt you. I must also be sorry because what *I did* was wrong. Humility is the honesty of acknowledging the sorrow that my wrongdoing caused. It is costly because our society tends to discount "wrongdoing" as a general concept and to deny it as a concept specific to relationships. Things just "happen" without anyone being at fault. Deep within, we all know the lie of that line of thinking. Forgiveness doesn't allow such a denial.

3. Forgiveness costs guilt carrying by the wronged person. There is no way to avoid it: if you hurt me, I will need to carry your guilt for you. Isn't that the basic theology of the cross in which Jesus, the pure Lamb of God, carries in his own body and spirit the sin of the impure world, of which I am part? Where condemnation was deserved, Jesus brought the grace of guilt carrying (Rom 6:23).

4. Finally, forgiveness costs two people a covenant of reconciliation in which both people are—on the basis of forgiveness, honesty, sorrow and guilt-carrying—willing to let go of the wrong and not hold it against the other. We restore the friendship as we agree together that the relationship is more important than the wrong or the pain; that our friendship is bigger than our pettiness or our hurt.

When I failed a friend some time ago, it wasn't a minor indiscretion, omission or petty faux pas; it was a betrayal of a deeply held and deeply shared trust. I betrayed a trust that was the concrete foundation of stable, solid friendship. It wasn't intentional, but it was stupid and wrong. I wasn't exactly caught red-handed, but my friend knew that something terribly wrong was happening.

There was a confrontation, followed by my admission of the wrong, followed by waiting—an agonizing time of the most painful, slow-moving days I have ever known. I waited for resolution—forgiveness or rejection, I didn't know which, though I knew which was deserved. When you betray trust you can't carry on with business as usual, not in the business of friendship.

A point of no return had occurred in our relationship just as it had when I climbed my first mountain. I remember the moment we clipped on our carabineers and roped up in teams of three. We stepped onto the glacier and crossed a mountain crevasse, a deep rift in the glacial plate. Everything changed—from a mountain hike to a mountain climb. It was the moment at which I could not turn back, a moment thick with consequences.

My choices in my friendship had transformed it. During those days of waiting I pondered the possible loss of the love of one on whom I depended for some of life's necessities—truth, encouragement, comfort, confidence giving, room to grow and love. What I felt then I now know was a form of premature grief; I was steeling myself against the possible death of friendship.

Where death was imminent, grace intervened; where rejection was deserved, forgiveness was given. Anger was expressed, a truth-filled and ever so righteous anger. Tears of confusion were cried, and costly words were first spoken, then lived, as they have been for nearly twenty years, "I forgive you." Costly, reconciling, transforming—that's forgiveness, and without it friends who fail friends lose friends.

How Do Friendships End?

I suppose there are as many ways by which our friendships come to an end as there are friendships. Here are five major means.

First, there is closure by unintentional withdrawal: we simply drift apart as activities and priorities change. We no longer go to the old places and no longer see each other in the natural settings of our lives. We fade out of each other's lives without ever meaning to.

Second, there is closure by intentional avoidance. We get hurt, mad, tired, bored or too busy and simply avoid spending time with our friend.

Third, there is closure by intentional analysis of the relationship. Together the friends agree that other priorities are more important and that "it's time to move on." We decide that other priorities are more pressing.

Fourth, there is closure by conflict. We have an argument about something important or trivial, but we just decide to call it quits. We fade out, we fall out, we opt out or we burn out.

Finally, closure sometimes comes to friendship when we refuse to give grace, forgiveness and mercy to one another. We carry a grudge that we will not release. We put a lid on the container of forgiveness and reconciliation is never accomplished. Letty Cottin Pogrebin offers two lists of significant questions for friends about to dissolve the relationship.

If you are the one ending the relationship, ask yourself:

☐ Have I been fair? Have I given my friend the benefit of the doubt? (Never dissolve a friendship on hearsay evidence.)

☐ Am I fed up with what the friend did or what the friend is?

☐ If there is no chance of reconciliation, have I been firm and clear about it so there can be no misunderstanding?

☐ Even though the parting is my choice, am I prepared to feel pangs of guilt and regret later?

If you are the accused and want to fight for the friendship, think about these questions:

☐ Am I able to acknowledge my mistakes or explain my actions without defensiveness or rancor?

☐ Should I do it by phone, in writing or in person? On my turf or my friend's? In a public place or in a private setting?

☐ Do I really want to make up, or do I want to get back together so I can take revenge?

☐ If I resolve to change, can I keep my promise?

☐ Can my friend and I learn to disagree on some things and still get along, or is it just a matter of time until we have another major blowup?

☐ How many rejections will convince me to let the friendship go?[6]

Study Questions

1. Are you and your friends more likely to be dishonest or to forgive?

2. When was the last time a friend forgave you? What were the setting and the point of conflict?

3. When was the last time you forgave a friend? What were the setting and the point of conflict?

4. What have you learned about forgiveness in the past six months?

5. Is there a friend you need to forgive right now? What's keeping you from taking care of it?

Eight

Friendships That Last

The best mirror is an old friend.
PROVERB

Friendships that last go deep.

RECENTLY I FOUND MYSELF WONDERING OUT LOUD about something I had never considered. *Jesus is my teacher for prayer, spirituality, discipleship and truth. Is he also my teacher for friend making?* Have you ever thought of Jesus as someone's "best friend"? Have you ever considered that Jesus might be our best example of an effective and deep friend? I will confess to you that it never crossed my mind until I began to work on this book. As I did my research I asked myself, "Which are the great friendships of the Bible? Whose friendships illustrate profound truth in a way that transcends the moments of their history?" And there it was—staring me down and demanding my attention: Jesus was a great friend to Peter!

All of our biblical perspectives for deep friendships can be recognized in the relationship between Peter and Jesus:

1. unmasking his truest identity

2. choosing to give intentional loyalty to Peter and inviting him to share hospitality as one of the Twelve

3. walking through seasons of faith and unfaith, growth and setbacks

4. listening

5. encouraging

6. failing and forgiving

All of these Jesus experienced as he walked the roads of Galilee with his friend, Peter. It is true, they shared some things in common that helped them move into friendship quickly and well: a common heritage as Jews, a similar geography and social class, and a dream for a future kingdom in which God would reign. But one thing more was needed to make their friendship thrive, perspective number seven: *friendships that last go deep*.

Peter was never content to stand on the sidelines watching the game; he wanted to jump into the thick of it. The picture of Peter given to us by historical tradition is one of passion, conviction, heat and energy—not always a man of thoughtful or careful reflection, but a man of impulse and raw energy, a man of incredible passion. That passion translated into faith as Peter alone of the disciples stepped from the boat to walk to Jesus on the sea he had fished all of his days. That passion translated into his impulsive offer to build Jesus, Elijah and Moses tabernacles on the Mount of Transfiguration. That passion translated into his brash declaration of Jesus' lordship followed immediately by Jesus' denunciation of Peter as a hindrance to the kingdom of God. That passion translated into the reckless impulse to defend his friend with his sword in one moment and to deny him with his words just hours later. Scan the pages of New Testament Scripture and Peter is there—in foreground or background, but he is there at or near Jesus' side until the awful moment of denial, betrayal and disloyalty on the night Jesus was taken prisoner by Pilate's men. Wherever Jesus went, Peter was never far away.

Peter was part of the inner circle.

Everyone has an inner circle of friends whose opinions matter the most and whose insights are most cherished and trusted. For Jesus it was the intense trio of Peter, James and John, three fishermen whose actions spoke eloquently though their words were often confused and misguided. This inner circle was the group Jesus took aside for special times of teaching, fellowship and support. A small handful of people in our lives are candidates for that inner circle of most trusted, most "necessary" friends. I call this inner circle my "soul friends" because they alone know and share the secrets of my soul, though it's not easy or natural for me to disclose or "unmask" myself to others. I first learned the phrase "soul friend" from a book by Kenneth Leech bearing that name. A soul friend is one whose concern goes far beyond the superficial and banal issues of "everyday life." Soul friends want to go deep with others—deep into issues of the spirit or soul. Soul friends want to help you see the deeply spiritual texture in the seemingly trivial events of life. Soul friends take you deeper than you can ever go on your own.

Going deep is not automatic with the passing of time. Because we are "old" friends does not mean we are "soul friends" or even "good friends." I may have known the local United Parcel Service driver for years but we aren't necessarily close friends. I can know a waitress at a familiar old restaurant and not be good friends with her. Time spent or history shared, by itself, is not an evidence of depth. There are concrete actions required to go deep as soul friends.

The Need for More

Going deep requires more of everything we've called the biblical perspectives of friendship: more unmasking, more intentional loyalty, more listening, more time, more truthful and trustful communication, and often more forgiveness because the stakes are higher than ever. Soul friendship is more than casual, functional or circumstantial friendship. It is deeply spiritual and intensely personal, which probably explains why it is so rare. It is "soul hospitality," creating a free and open space, a doorway into the private places of the heart and soul. It happens when I invite you, as a familiar stranger, into my most protected inner home. I welcome you, as the known but unknown one, into the place where we can tell our stories without fear of rejection.

My favorite scene in the movie *Dead Poets Society* is set in a cave, where a group of young prep-school boys begin to tell stories and sing songs to one another. In a spontaneous and fleeting moment in time, they share a unique experience of poetry, fantasy and trust. They reach deeply into each other's private hearts, if only for a moment. Soul-friends are those who remove the veil which covers and protects our delicate and fragile spirits. We go deep only as we learn to tell each other our stories and reveal our unmasked selves.

Soul-friends believe in the whole person and are just as anxious to know about heart and soul as about emotions and body. Did you ever notice how much we concentrate our conversations on our bodies and emotions? We ask, "How are you today?" "How are you feeling?" "Did you get a good sleep?" Soul-friends also ask questions about the condition of the heart and soul. An African question, one of my favorites, asks, "Are you at peace?" It asks about something far more significant than my physical state. I had a friend once whose standard question was "Is it well with your soul?" It was a question that annoyed me at the time because I had no good answers for him and I felt like he was intrusive with it, but I now have developed soul-friendships with people who ask me questions like that and make me glad for the love it gives. Too often we settle for the safe, superficial and shallow. I find that many people settle for dehydrated and malnourished relationships because they accept superficial conversations when they really desire deep and rich conversations.

This summer I traveled by train from Seattle to Vancouver, British Columbia. It was a beautiful trip north to Canada along stretches of Puget Sound, through the Skagit Valley and the North Cascade Mountains. I was excited for the return trip to see it all from the opposite vista but unfortunately our train derailed shortly after leaving the depot in British Columbia and we were shuttled back to Seattle's King Street station by bus. Because we all shared a common trauma—an unexpected change in travel plans—we "joined" together more personally and quickly. Conversations were animated and more intense than I had noticed on the northward journey a week earlier. All the way back to Seattle my seatmate and I talked energetically and personally about jobs, families, decisions and future plans. The setting was unusual and the circumstances unique, but it made me wonder: am I more ready to go deep with a stranger than my closest friends?

You have friends, don't you, whom you want to know all the deepest truth about what is most intensely important to you, those feelings and impulses which both shape and drive your life? Or perhaps you long for someone with whom you can mine the riches of each other's lives.

How much of your conversations settle for "the big three" of daily conversation?

☐ gossip talk ("Did I tell you about x and y?")

☐ travelogue talk ("Did I tell you where I went?")

☐ Day-Timer talk ("Did I tell you about my day at work?")

Soul-friend talk includes both faith-talk and idea-talk in their normal ebb and flow of conversations—talk which is enriched by a kingdom perspective and which seeks to wrestle with truth questions. Soul-friend conversation is sacramental for it sees the deep spiritual meaning in the tapestry of daily events. It isn't always about "spiritual" or "religious" matters but it reaches deeply into the meaning of every event, experience or issue of life.

What would change in your life if your questions to your friends included questions of the soul? Simply put, soul-friends are people who together share friendship with God as the intentional and cohesive basis for their relationship. Because their friendship with God is essential to their own identity, their lives actively integrate "faith conversations" as a necessary part of their ongoing relationships. Such conversations question, explore and see every life experience through the lens of biblical faith in ways that energize each other's souls. "Friendship with God" can also be expressed as "discipleship" or "the Christian walk."

I have been fascinated in recent years that the language of "soul" has reemerged in the conversation about spirituality; for many years the term was considered passé by those who preferred newer language about spiritual formation, spiritual development and spiritual growth. Soul, however, is a concept dense enough to carry the deepest meanings of the heart. In *The Pilgrim's Progress*, Christiana and her friends experience this soul friendship on their journey: "They seemed to be a terror one to the other; for that they could not see that glory each one on herself which they could see in each other. Now, therefore, they began to esteem each other better than themselves. 'For you are fairer than I am,' said one; and 'You are more comely than I am,' said another."[1]

The independence and privatism of American culture today is a masquerade that hides our deepest need for intimacy with another person. Christiana and her friends discovered an essential need, the need for intimacy with others, and valued each more highly than they esteemed themselves. The student world in which I work grossly misinterprets that hunger for intimacy as a desire for sexual closeness. That is not the intimacy of soul friendship; it may be a cheap diversion and nothing more. But hunger for intimacy is not exclusively the need of a younger population. Intimacy of spirit is a common human need. Paul

Tournier wrote,

> Listen to all the conversations of our world, those between nations as well as between couples. They are for the most part dialogues of the deaf. Exceedingly few exchanges of viewpoints manifest a real desire to understand the other person. No one can live a full life without feeling understood by at least one person. Misunderstood she loses self-confidence, she loses her faith in life, or even in God. Here is an even greater mystery: no one comes to know him or herself through introspection, or in the solitude of his or her personal diary. He who would see himself clearly, she who would see herself clearly, must open up to a confidant, freely chosen and worthy of such trust.[2]

The Passion of the Heart

Intimacy is the sharing of the passion of the heart. One writer has said, "Anyone without a soul friend is a body without a head." Friendships that run deep know a shared history of the heart, as well as a common calendar of months and years. To go deep means that what moves my soul will be shared with you, either because I *must* tell you about it or because you know me so well you simply know it in the passing of time together.

I used to think that mature friends always talked of deep things, profound things, consequential things; now I know that it is the friendship itself that makes things deep and profound and consequential. One of the great privileges of working with college students is my daily exposure to the energy and excitement of their youth. I met today in the morning with Tanya and we talked about her passionate dreams for her future. Later I spoke with Jon and listened to his passion for the kingdom of God. We don't have to force those conversations because they are a natural byproduct of our common commitment to Jesus and to one another. "Kingdom talk" spills over naturally from a cup filled with a shared passion for friendship with God and one another.

Transparent Communication

When I was a young seminary student I was greatly influenced by John Powell's book *Why Am I Afraid to Tell You Who I Am?* I remember walking past it in a bookstore and nearly tripping over my own feet as I turned around in stunned amazement and took it down from the shelf. I was agitated by it because its title broadcast the most secretly felt question in my soul: *Why am I afraid to tell you who I am?* I stood in the aisle and read the title again and again, feeling the flush of embarrassment on my face. I felt as if my own private journal was now being published for the world to read. It asked a question that I wasn't ready to ask then and publicly suggested that fear was part of the answer.

Powell identifies five levels of communication:

☐ The cliché level is small talk. The level of risk is low, the content is superficial. "Did you see last night's game?"

☐ The fact level reveals information or personal competence, it tells others what you know. Again, the level of risk is low although the content may be more complex.

☐ The opinion level shares what you think, usually about safe topics or impersonal issues.

☐ The emotional level takes a major step toward transparency and vulnerability because you tell others what you feel. It has to do with dreams and fears, pain and passions, joy and sorrow. When I communicate at this level, I begin to unmask and give you part of who I am.

☐ The transparent level requires enormous trust and involves the greatest amount of risk to my own self-protection.

Reflect back on the past twenty-fours of your life. What kind of listening did you do with your friends? What percentage of levels one through four? When was the last time you practiced level-five listening?

In essence, James told the early Christians they needed to move past the first three levels when he said, "confess your sins one to another." It is not that I must learn to trust you and then confess to you, but rather in the confession I will learn to trust you with my heart. Confession is still another form of telling the truth, this time about myself. The motivation is not always shame or guilt or to absolve myself of horrible things I have done or felt or thought; instead, it may be that I declare my humanness to another person who can mirror his humanness back to me in order that we will remind each other of the importance of our flawed humanity, that we are created in God's image, *for the sake of others*. We exist to offer the hospitality of friendship across cultural, economic, religious, racial, age and gender lines. If we are to be known by our love, then deep friendships are to be a Christian's way of life. In a world that seems increasingly mean-spirited, isolated, cold and indifferent, the hospitality of friendship is sorely needed.

On the 10,000 Maniacs album *Blind Man's Zoo*, Natalie Merchant's words invite honest and costly communication.

Trouble me, disturb me with all your cares and your worries.
Trouble me on the days when you feel spent.
Why let your shoulders bend underneath this burden when my back is sturdy and strong.
Trouble me.

Speak to me, don't mislead me, the calm I feel means a storm is swelling;
There's no telling where it starts or how it ends.
Speak to me, why are you building this thick brick wall to defend me when your silence is my greatest fear?
Why let your shoulders bend underneath this burden when my back is sturdy and strong?
Speak to me . . .

Spare me? Don't spare me anything troubling.
Trouble me, disturb me with all your cares and your worries.
Speak to me and let our words build a shelter from the storm.
Lastly, let me know what I can mend.
There's more, honestly, than my sweet friend, you can see.
Trust is what I'm offering if you trouble me.[3]

Soul-friends are not content to relegate conversations to small talk, information and emotions but push the curtains back on the windows of honesty and transparency of the soul.

In my imagination I see Jesus and Peter deeply engaged in conversation about the kingdom as Jesus helped Peter see the important role he would need to play as its first significant apostolic leader. I see them arguing and debating the kingdom and I see them helping each other sustain the courage and confidence needed to carry out their tasks. I also see them thinking aloud about Peter's family and Jesus' relationship with his family. I see Peter ask Jesus to tutor him in prayer, even as Peter shows Jesus some of the fine points of fishing. They certainly had much to discuss after Peter's failed attempt at walking on the water, his futile request to build tents on the Mount of Transfiguration, his bravado on the Mount of Olives including cutting off the servant's ear, his denial of Jesus in the courtyard, his visit to the Garden of Resurrection. Peter and Jesus did not merely have a functional relationship as teacher-pupil; their friendship went deep.

Paying Spiritual Attention

Randy and Susan are friends I have known for more than a decade. We have shared significant times of conversation as we have sought to listen to God in each other's lives. There is no one I know who does that better for me. At the wedding of another friend we walked the grounds of the banquet hall and talked. I told them that I needed their friendship because they care to hold me spiritually accountable in a way no others did. I have lots of people who hold me accountable for my work performance and my professional development. I am held accountable in numerous ways for my relationships and personal growth. Randy and Susan are two among very few who ask me about my spiritual growth and development. Within five minutes of seeing them, they are pressing me for information about my spirit.

Randy took me aside once and said to me in his own inimitable way, "Listen, you big lug, I look up to you. You are important to me as a model for my life of faith, so don't screw up!"

He is a Barnabas to me as he speaks in ways only he can, but he is a Peter to me too—one with whom I love to mine the depths in our common love for the kingdom of God. I don't know if you have such friends but they are infinitely worth the risks and costs. Wendy Miller writes that "spiritual friends are people who pay attention, with another person, to the presence and the movement of God in that person's life; and to the response the other person is making to God, to him or herself, to others, and to God's creation."[4]

Going deep means we will learn to pay attention to God's movement in our lives. My personal definition of spirituality is "learning to pay attention to God's presence in everything we do." Miller says, "Bits of the holy are embedded in the everyday, but most of us fail to recognize our encounter with God for what it is. We may think such meetings only happen at church, rather than in the supermarket, in our backyard, or while we are waiting for transportation."[5]

I started this book by talking about hospitality as a metaphor for friendship, of creating space for another to be welcomed and at home in your presence. Going deep means creating a place of hospitality to be shared not only with another person, but with God. "Where two or three are gathered in my name, I am there among them" (Mt 18:20). It is intensely spiritual because it is anchored in a triangle of friendship with God and another person; three parties connected to one another in unique and distinctive ways. In Ecclesiastes 4:12, the writer talks about the strength of soul-friends: "And though one might prevail against another, two will withstand one. A threefold cord is not quickly broken."

Going Deep

Wendy Miller offers a wonderful list of questions for personal reflection and for shared reflection with a soul-friend:

What is my prayer experience like?

What happens when I pray or meditate on Scripture?

What areas of my life is God touching?

How am I experiencing God's grace?

What is God like for me — in Scripture, in times of prayer, or at other times?

How have I cooperated with God this week (month)?

What am I not bringing openly before God? (e.g., anger, fear)

Where have I missed experiencing God's grace or love?

What do I need to confess?

What is changing within me as I listen to God?

What attitudes am I experiencing as I relate to others in my life?[6]

Through conversations such as these we will tell our stories to a trusted friend who is willing to provide what we need most in life: a sense of welcome.

What kind of person is a good soul-friend?

☐ someone willing to relate all of life to our journey with God

☐ someone who is able to listen attentively

☐ someone whom you trust

☐ someone who has shown some evidence of trustworthiness

☐ someone with a sense of humor

☐ someone who is teachable, willing to learn

☐ someone who is willing to ask any and all questions

☐ someone interested in the whole person—spirit and soul, as well as body and mind

For more than a decade Dr. Kirby Wilcoxson and I have taught a course on urban ministry in the city of Chicago. We started the course when we worked together at the same college and have now taken several hundred students through a carefully constructed introduction to city and urban ministry. When I left that campus, the course was in jeopardy but we found a way to continue it as a joint program of our two schools.

It seems to have a special life of its own. Students' lives are deeply affected by the days we spend visiting ghetto neighborhoods of Chicago and listening to presentations by many practitioners of urban ministry. Nearly every year for the past ten we have met in Chicago for several weeks in the sometimes bitterly cold weather of January. The course is often intense and sometimes emotional for the students, so the learning stakes are high. I can honestly say today that it is the single most important thing I do in my work with students. Each year I arrive at the sixth floor of the International Conference Center in Uptown Chicago with high anticipation and excitement.

I used to think the course content was the reason for that excitement. It is taught in an unconventional way, far from campus, on-site in neighborhoods of need. Its methodology creates actively involved immersion experiences in many urban neighborhoods. I used to believe it was the intensity of emotion and learning that energized me for the weeks in Chicago. That too is a factor but more important than any of these things is the simple fact that I get time with a man who values language, loves to think out loud, drinks coffee and drives six hundred miles one way so we can talk as soul-friends. We have learned to peer together into the windows of the kingdom because we have dared to peer together into the windows of our own souls. If the course was ever canceled, I believe we would meet for a couple of weeks every January anyway in order to share our friendship. We have competed hard against one another in athletic contests (he has usually won). We have disagreed on points of politics and theology (I am usually right). We have faced trauma over students together and seasons of transition and change in our lives and we have done it—not merely as brothers in Christ—but as soul-friends who have learned to risk friendship.

Buechner says,

What we hunger for perhaps more than anything else is to be known in our full humanness, and yet that is often just what we also fear more than anything else. It is important to tell at least from time to time the secret of who we truly and fully are . . . because otherwise we run the risk of losing track of who we truly and fully are and little by little come to accept instead the highly edited version which we put forth in hope that the world will find it more acceptable then the real thing.[7]

Study Questions

1. Define the term *soul-friend*. Do you have one in your life?

2. To whom do you confess your sins?

3. What difference do you think it would make if you could meet regularly with a friend to talk about your spiritual journeys together?

4. What questions would you add to the list from Wendy Miller?

5. How do you react to Buechner's quote?

Notes

Chapter 1: The Hospitality of Friendship
[1]Alan Jones, *Soulmaking* (San Francisco: Harper & Row, 1985), pp. 154-55.
[2]Frederick Buechner, *Whistling in the Dark: An ABC Theologized* (San Francisco: Harper & Row, 1988), pp. 49-50.
[3]Henri J. M. Nouwen, *Reaching Out* (Garden City, N.Y.: Doubleday, 1975), p. 46.

Chapter 2: If You Really Knew Me
[1]Jerry White and Mary White, *Friends and Friendship* (Colorado Springs, Colo.: NavPress, 1982), p. 37.
[2]Letty Cottin Pogrebin, *Among Friends* (New York: McGraw-Hill, 1987), p. 253.
[3]Ibid., pp. 253-78.
[4]Ibid., pp. 261, 263.
[5]Nouwen, *Reaching Out*, p. 19.

Chapter 3: My Door Is Always Open to You
[1]Joyce Hollyday, *Clothed with the Sun* (Louisville, Ky.: Westminster John Knox, 1994), p. 14.
[2]M. Scott Peck, *The Road Less Traveled* (New York: Simon & Schuster, 1978), p. 111.
[3]C. S. Lewis, *The Four Loves* (New York: Harcourt Brace, 1960), pp. 66-67.
[4]Kathleen Norris, *Dakota* (Boston: Houghton Mifflin, 1993), p. 23.
[5]Nouwen, *Reaching Out*, p. 51.
[6]Lewis, *Four Loves*, pp. 89-90.

Chapter 4: "Somebody Nobody Knows"
[1]Stu Weber, *Locking Arms* (Sisters, Ore.: Multnomah Books, 1995), pp. 132-33.
[2]Mary Rose O'Reilly, "Deep Listening: An Experimental Friendship," *Weavings*, May/June 1994, p. 19.
[3]Stephen R. Covey, *Seven Habits of Highly Effective People* (New York: Simon &

Schuster, 1989), p. 240.
[4]Bruce Larson, *No Longer Strangers* (Waco, Tex.: Word, 1971), pp. 98-100.
[5]Douglas Steere, *Gleanings: A Random Harvest, Selected Writings* (Nashville: Upper Room, 1986).
[6]Nouwen, *Reaching Out*, p. 70.

Chapter 5: The Seasons of Friendship
[1]Paula Ripple, *Called to Be Friends* (Notre Dame, Ind.: Ave Maria, 1980), pp. 91-92, 94, 96.
[2]Alan Loy McGinnis, *The Friendship Factor* (Minneapolis: Augsburg, 1979), p. 23.
[3]Kahlil Gibran, *The Prophet* (New York: Knopf, 1927), p. 50.
[4]Margaret Guenther, *Holy Listening: The Art of Spiritual Direction* (Cambridge, Mass.: Cowley, 1992), p. 11.
[5]Ibid., p. 12.
[6]Ken Gire Jr., *Windows of the Soul* (Grand Rapids, Mich.: Zondervan, 1996), p. 23.

Chapter 6: Iron Sharpens Iron
[1]Lewis, *Four Loves*, pp. 79-80.
[2]David J. Garrow, *Bearing the Cross* (New York: Vintage Books, 1988), p. 58.
[3]Martin Luther King Jr., *Strength to Love* (Philadelphia: Fortress Press, 1963), pp. 125-26.

Chapter 7: Friends Fail Friends
[1]In Paula J. Carlson and Peter S. Hawkins, ed., *Listening for God* (Minneapolis: Augsburg Fortress, 1994), p. 54.
[2]Frederick Buechner, *Wishful Thinking: A Theological ABC* (New York: Harper & Row, 1973), p. 29.
[3]Walter Wangerin, *As for Me and My House* (Nashville: Thomas Nelson, 1990), p. 79. Quoted by permission of Thomas Nelson Publishers.
[4]Ibid., pp. 90-91.
[5]Quoted in McGinnis, *Friendship Factor*, p. 68.
[6]Pogrebin, *Among Friends*, pp. 103-104.

Chapter 8: Friendships That Last
[1]John Bunyan, *The Pilgrim's Progress* (New York: Grosset & Dunlap, n.d.), p. 234.
[2]Paul Tournier, *To Understand Each Other* (Richmond, Va.: John Knox, 1967), pp. 8-9.
[3]Natalie Merchant, "Trouble Me," on *Blind Man's Zoo* by 10,000 Maniacs, 1989 Elektra/Asylum Records, Christian Burial Music, ASCAP.
[4]Wendy Miller, *Learning to Listen* (Nashville: Upper Room, 1993), p. 12.
[5]Ibid., pp. 15-16.
[6]Ibid.
[7]Frederick Buechner, *Telling Secrets* (San Francisco: HarperCollins, 1991), pp. 2-3.